COMHAIRLE CHONTAE ÁTHA CLIATH THEAS

SOUTH DUBLIN COUNTY LIBRARIES

LUCAN LIBRARY
TO RENEW ANY ITEM TEL: 621 6422
OR ONLINE AT www.southdublinlibraries.ie

Items should be returned on or before the last date below. Fines,
as displayed in the Library, will be charged on overdue items.

;,

rld

mpics

y,

ial

BOOKS LLC

D0234754

Publication Data:

Title: Special Olympics

Subtitle: Eunice Kennedy Shriver, Special Olympics, Sargent Shriver, State Farm Holiday Classic, Timothy Shriver, 2003 Special Olympics World Summer Games, Estonia at the Special Olympics World Games, Special Olympics New Jersey, Special Olympics World Games, 2011 Special Olympics World Summer Games

Published by: Books LLC, Memphis, Tennessee, USA in 2010

Copyright (chapters): http://creativecommons.org/licenses/by-sa/3.0

Online edition: http://booksllc.net/?q=Category:Special_Olympics

Contact the publisher: http://booksllc.net/contactus.cfm

Limit of Liability/Disclaimer of Warranty:
The publisher makes no representations or warranties with respect to the accuracy or completeness of the book. The information in the book may not be suitable for your situation. You should consult with a professional where appropriate. The publisher is not liable for any damages resulting from the book.

CONTENTS

Introduction   v

1968 Special Olympics World Summer Games   1

1995 Special Olympics World Summer Games   3

1999 Special Olympics World Summer Games   5

2003 Special Olympics World Summer Games   7

2005 Special Olympics World Winter Games   11

2007 Special Olympics World Summer Games   13

2008 Fultondale Wildcats Special Olympics Season   15

2009 Special Olympics World Winter Games   17

2011 Special Olympics World Summer Games   19

A Very Special Acoustic Christmas   21

A Very Special Christmas (album)   23

A Very Special Christmas (series)   25

A Very Special Christmas 2   29

A Very Special Christmas 3   31

A Very Special Christmas 5   33
A Very Special Christmas 7   35
A Very Special Christmas Live   37
Anne M. Burke   39
Estonia at the Special Olympics World Games   41
Eunice Kennedy Shriver   45
Flame of Hope   53
Healthy Athletes   55
Law Enforcement Torch Run   57
Mexico at the Special Olympics World Games   61
Sargent Shriver   63
Special Olympics   71
Special Olympics Canada   75
Special Olympics Great Britain   79
Special Olympics Leicester   81
Special Olympics New Jersey   83
Special Olympics USA   87
Special Olympics World Games   89
State Farm Holiday Classic   93
Timothy Shriver   101

Index   105

Introduction

The online edition of this book is at http://booksllc.net/?q=Category:Special%5FOlympics. It's hyperlinked and may be updated. Where we have recommended related pages, you can read them at http://booksllc.net/?q= followed by the page's title. Most entries in the book's index also have a dedicated page at http://booksllc.net/?q= followed by the index entry.

Each chapter in this book ends with a URL to a hyperlinked online version. Use the online version to access related pages, websites, footnote URLs. You can click the history tab on the online version to see a list of the chapter's contributors. While we have included photo captions in the book, due to copyright restrictions you can only view the photos online. You also need to go to the online edition to view some formula symbols.

The online version of this book is part of Wikipedia, a multilingual, web-based encyclopedia.

Wikipedia is written collaboratively. Since its creation in 2001, Wikipedia has grown rapidly into one of the largest reference web sites, attracting nearly 68 million visitors monthly. There are more than 91,000 active contributors working on more than 15 million articles in more than 270 languages. Every day, hundreds of thousands of active from around the world collectively make tens of thousands of edits and create thousands of new articles.

After a long process of discussion, debate, and argument, articles gradually take on a neutral point of view reached through consensus. Additional editors expand and contribute to articles and strive to achieve balance and comprehensive coverage. Wikipedia's intent is to cover existing knowledge which is verifiable from other sources. The ideal Wikipedia article is well-written, balanced, neutral, and encyclopedic, containing comprehensive, notable, verifiable knowledge.

Wikipedia is open to a large contributor base, drawing a large number of editors from diverse backgrounds. This allows Wikipedia to significantly reduce regional and cultural bias found in many other publications, and makes it very difficult for any group to censor and impose bias. A large, diverse editor base also provides access and breadth on subject matter that is otherwise inaccessible or little documented.

Think you can improve the book? If so, simply go to the online version and suggest changes. If accepted, your additions could appear in the next edition!

1

1968 SPECIAL OLYMPICS WORLD SUMMER GAMES

The *First* **International Special Olympics Games** (Summer Special Olympics) were held in Soldier Field, Chicago, Illinois.

These were the very first Special Olympics world games. They were held In Chicago, ILL. at Soldier Field.

1000 athletes from 26 states, and Canada competed in track and swimming. Swimming included 25 meter races, and track had short distance runnings, ball throws, and standing long jump.

The athlete's oath was introduced at these games by founder Eunice Shriver at the opening ceremony. The oath is," Let me win. But if I can not win, let me be brave in the attempt."

A hyperlinked version of this chapter is at http://booksllc.net?q=1968%5FSpecial%5FOlympics%5FWorld%5FSummer%5FGames

2

1995 SPECIAL OLYMPICS WORLD SUMMER GAMES

The Ninth Special Olympics World Summer Games were held in New Haven, Connecticut, USA on July 1-9 1995. More than 7,000 athletes from 143 countries gathered for competition in 21 sports. The opening and closing ceremonies were held in the Yale Bowl, and various events were held around the New Haven area, including various events held in West Haven, Connecticut. This was the first Special olympics world games that included unified sports. The hurdles and the marathon were included in athletics, squat lift was included in powerlifting, and the 40 km race was included in cycling.

Here are some notable athetes of these games:

- ○ Troy Rutter - won the first-ever marathon in 2:59.18.
- ○ Kamala Gesteland - won 3 gold medals and 2 bronze medals in swimming.
- ○ Holly Mandy - won the mile run and the 3 km run, also won silver medal in the half-marathon. (She also won a silver medal in the 5 km run at the 1991 world games.)
- ○ Loretta Claiborne - won 2 gold medals in bowling events.
- ○ Conrad DuPreez - won 2 gold medals in cycling.
- ○ Chad Kocabinski - won a gold and a bronze medals in horse riding events.

○ Robert Vasquez - won 1 gold, 4 silver, and 1 bronze medals in gymnastics.
○ Gabriel Salas - won gold and bronze medals in speed roller skating.
○ Cynthia Bentley - won a silver medal in tennis.
○ Jennifer R Delaney- won two gold and one silver medal in Equestrian

Sports

○ Aquatics
○ Athletics (track and field)
○ Badminton
○ Basketball
○ Bocce
○ Bowling
○ Cycling
○ Equestrian
○ Football (Soccer)
○ Golf
○ Gymnastics
○ Powerlifting
○ Roller Skating
○ Softball
○ Table Tennis
○ Tennis
○ Volleyball

Websites (URLs online)

○ Special Olympics

A hyperlinked version of this chapter is at http://booksllc.net?q=1995%5FSpecial%
5FOlympics%5FWorld%5FSummer%5FGames

1999 SPECIAL OLYMPICS WORLD SUMMER GAMES

1999 Special Olympics World Summer Games

- o Host city: Raleigh, North Carolina
- o Nations participating: 150
- o Athletes participating: 7,000+
- o Events: 19 sports
- o Opening ceremony: June 26, 1999
- o Closing ceremony: July 4, 1999
- o Officially opened by: Billy Crystal and Stevie Wonder
- o Main Stadium: Carter-Finley Stadium (opening ceremony)

The **1999 Special Olympics World Summer Games** were held in Raleigh, Durham, and Chapel Hill in North Carolina, United States between June 26 and July 4, 1999. The events in 19 sports were predominantly held on the campuses of North Carolina State University, the University of North Carolina at Chapel Hill, and North Carolina Central University.

Events

Special Olympics.

- Aquatics (Chapel Hill)
- Athletics / track and field (Raleigh)
- Badminton (Durham)
- Basketball (Chapel Hill and Durham)
- Bocce (Pittsboro)
- Bowling (Raleigh)
- Cycling (Garner)
- Equestrian (Raleigh)
- Football / soccer (Raleigh)
- Golf (Durham and Cary)
- Gymnastics (Raleigh)
- Handball (Raleigh)
- Powerlifting (Raleigh)
- Roller skating (Raleigh)
- Sailing (Maryland coast)
- Softball (Raleigh)
- Table tennis (Chapel Hill)
- Tennis (Chapel Hill)
- Volleyball (Chapel Hill)

Websites (URLs online)

- Special Olympics

A hyperlinked version of this chapter is at http://booksllc.net?q=1999%5FSpecial%5FOlympics%5FWorld%5FSummer%5FGames

4

2003 SPECIAL OLYMPICS WORLD SUMMER GAMES

11th Special Olympics World Summer Games

- Host city: Dublin, Ireland
- Events: 23 sports
- Opening ceremony: June 21
- Closing ceremony: June 29
- Officially opened by: Mary McAleese
- Main Stadium: Croke Park

The **2003 Special Olympics World Summer Games** were hosted in Ireland, with participants staying in various host towns around the island in the lead up to the games before moving to Dublin for the events. Events were held from 21 June-29 June 2003 at many venues including Morton Stadium, the Royal Dublin Society, the National Basketball Arena, all in Dublin. Croke Park served as the central stadium for the opening and closing ceremonies, even though no competitions took place there. Belfast was the venue for roller skating events (at the Kings Hall), as well as the Special Olympics Scientific Symposium (held from 19-20 June).

Host town programme

177 towns, cities and villages and the Aran Islands hosted national delegations in the run up to the games. Each town ran programmes to educate the local community about the customs of the country they would host and provided facilities for the teams to acclimatise. Newbridge, County Kildare, host to the Japan delegation won the award for best host town.

Volunteer programme

Online image: Iraqi athletes departing Dublin after the 2003 Special Olympics World Games

30,000 volunteer officials and support staff assisted in the running of the games, including 900 staff of the Bank of Ireland who coordinated the host town programme and 800 members of the Irish Defence Forces who maintained the radio communication network, and provided support for bridge building, security duties, VIP drivers, standard bearers for ceremonial events and emergency medical teams. 165 volunteers from the then 15 countries of the EU took part in a European Volunteer Project (EVS), the first ever to be organized in event-related mode. The volunteers are commemorated by having their names on a series of plaques situated in Dublin Castle, just outside the Chester Beatty Library.

The Games

The 2003 World Games were the first to be held outside of the United States. Approximately 7000 athletes from 150 countries competed in the games in 18 official disciplines, and three exhibition sports. The participants from Kosovo were the region's first team at an international sporting event. A 12-member team from Iraq received special permission to attend the games, despite ongoing war in their home nation.

Online image: The crowd at the 2003 Special Olympics World Games Opening Ceremonies in Croke Park, Dublin , Ireland as Team USA enters the stadium

The opening ceremony was held in Croke Park featured an array of stars and was hosted by Patrick Kielty. The band U2 were a major feature, and Nelson Mandela officially opened the games. Other performances included The Corrs and the largest Riverdance troupe ever assembled on one stage. 75,000 athletes and spectators were in attendance at the opening ceremonies. Irish and international celebrities such as Arnold Schwarzenegger and Jon Bon Jovi walked with the athletes, with Muhammad Ali as a special guest and Manchester United and Republic of Ireland football player Roy Keane taking the athletes oath with one of the Special Olympians.

The Games Flame was lit at the culmination of the Law Enforcement Torch Run, which more than 2,000 members of An Garda Síochána (Irish Police) and the Police Service of Northern Ireland took part in. This was a series of relays carrying the Special Olympics Torch, the "Flame of Hope", from Europe to the Games' official opening.

Online image: 2003 Special Olympics commemorative coin issued by the Central Bank of Ireland

The ceremony was officially opened by President of Ireland Mary McAleese and attended by Taoiseach (Prime Minister of Ireland) Bertie Ahern.

The 2003 games were the first to have their opening and closing schemes broadcast on live television, and Radio Telefís Éireann provided extensive coverage of the events through their 'Voice of the Games' radio station which replaced RTÉ Radio 1 on Medium Wave for the duration of the event. There was also a nightly television highlight programme.

Among the activities carried out during the Games were thorough medical checks on the athletes, some of whom had previously undiagnosed conditions uncovered, as some of the athletes came from countries with limited medical facilities or had difficulty communicating their symptoms.

A daily newspaper, the Games Gazette was published for each day of the games.

Among the contributors to the Games was the Irish Prison Service. Prisoners in Mountjoy Prison, Midlands Prison, Wheatfield Prison and Arbour Hill Prison who constructed podiums and made flags, towels, signs, benches and other equipment.

Organising Committee

The organising committee, which was formed in 1999 following the success of the bid, was chaired by entrepreneur Denis O'Brien. The chief executive was Mary Davis.

Events

Athletes and coaches such as Lleyton Hewitt and his coach Roger Rasheed (Tennis); Severiano Ballesteros, Sandy Lyle and Andrew Marshall (Golf), Mick O'Dwyer (Gaelic football) and Brian Kerr (Soccer) met and encouraged athletes at events during the games.

- o Aquatics (swimming)
- o Athletics (track and field)
- o Badminton
- o Basketball team

- Bocce
- Bowling
- Cycling
- Equestrian
- Football (soccer) team
- Golf
- Gymnastics (artistic)
- Gymnastics (rhythmic)
- Judo
- Kayaking
- MATP
- Pitch & putt
- Powerlifting
- Roller skating
- Sailing
- Table tennis
- Team handball
- Tennis
- Volleyball team

Websites (URLs online)

- 2003 World Games official website
- Host Town list
- Special Olympics 2003 Results
- Irish Prison Service release on their inmates work for the Special Olympics
- Special Olympics Ireland website

A hyperlinked version of this chapter is at http://booksllc.net?q=2003%5FSpecial%
5FOlympics%5FWorld%5FSummer%5FGames

5

2005 SPECIAL OLYMPICS WORLD WINTER GAMES

9th Special Olympics World Winter Games

- Host city: Nagano, Nagano, Japan
- Nations participating: 84
- Athletes participating: 2,600
- Events: 79 in 7 sports
- Opening ceremony: February 26
- Closing ceremony: March 5
- Officially opened by: Prime Minister Junichiro Koizumi
- Torch Lighter: Ryuya Kamihara
- Main Stadium: M-Wave

The 2005 Special Olympics Winter World Games were hosted at Nagano in Japan and were the first Special Olympics World Games held in Asia. Nagano became the first city in the world to host the Olympics, Paralympics and Special Olympics World Games.

Events

- Floor hockey
- Figure skating
- Speed skating
- Snowshoe
- Cross-country skiing
- Snowboarding
- Alpine skiing

Venues

- M-Wave - the opening, closing ceremonies and Speed skating
- Big Hat - Figure skating
- White Ring - Floor hockey
- Yamanouchi - Alpine skiing
- Hakuba - Cross-country
- Nozawaonsen - Snowshoe
- Mure - Snowboarding

See also (online edition)

- 1998 Winter Olympics
- 1998 Winter Paralympics

Websites (URLs online)

- 2005 Winter Special Olympics at Shinano Mainichi Shimbun
- 2005 Special Olympics World Winter Games

A hyperlinked version of this chapter is at http://booksllc.net?q=2005%5FSpecial%5FOlympics%5FWorld%5FWinter%5FGames

6

2007 SPECIAL OLYMPICS WORLD SUMMER GAMES

12th Special Olympics World Summer Games

- Host city: Shanghai, China
- Nations participating: 165
- Athletes participating: 7291
- Events: 25 sports
- Opening ceremony: October 2
- Closing ceremony: October 11
- Officially opened by: Hu Jintao
- Torch Lighter: Liu Xiang
- Main Stadium: Shanghai Stadium

The 2007 Special Olympics World Summer Games were held in Shanghai, China.

Events

- Aquatics
- Athletics (track and field)

- o Badminton
- o Basketball
- o Bocce
- o Bowling
- o Cycling
- o Equestrian
- o Floor Hockey
- o Football (Soccer)
- o Golf
- o Gymnastics
- o Judo
- o Kayaking
- o Powerlifting
- o Roller Skating
- o Sailing
- o Softball
- o Table Tennis
- o Team Handball
- o Tennis
- o Volleyball
- o Cricket
- o Dragon Boat
- o Dragon Lion
- o MATP

See also (online edition)

- o 2008 Summer Paralympics
- o 2009 Summer Deaflympics

Websites (URLs online)

- o 2007 Summer Special Olympics official site

A hyperlinked version of this chapter is at http://booksllc.net?q=2007%5FSpecial%
5FOlympics%5FWorld%5FSummer%5FGames

7

2008 FULTONDALE WILDCATS SPECIAL OLYMPICS SEASON

The **2008 Fultondale Wildcats Special Olympics Season** was the season in Jefferson County, Alabama.

Members

- Matthew Bayliss
- Zach Mussen
- Shronda Gooden
- Kelsi Moore
- Denisha Turnipseed
- Johnathan Wells

Events

Matthew Bayliss

Event: Date: Place: Location

- Track and Field: October 16, 2008: 1st Place and 3rd Place: Fultondale High School
- Halloween Dance: October 31, 2008: : Mountain Chapel
- Volleyball Tournament: November 14, 2008: 3rd Place: Fultondale High School
- Bowling: January 12, 2009: 2nd Place: Oak Mountain Lanes
- Basketball: January 23, 2009: 3rd Place: Birmingham Southern College
- Soccer: March 26, 2009: 3rd place: Sportsblast of Shelby County

See also (online edition)

Fultondale Wildcats

A hyperlinked version of this chapter is at http://booksllc.net?q=2008%
5FFultondale%5FWildcats%5FSpecial%5FOlympics%5FSeason

8

2009 SPECIAL OLYMPICS WORLD WINTER GAMES

10th Special Olympics World Winter Games

- o Host city: Boise, Idaho, United States
- o Nations participating: >100
- o Athletes participating: 2500
- o Events: -
- o Opening ceremony: February 7
- o Closing ceremony: February 13
- o Officially opened by: -
- o Torch Lighter: -
- o Main Stadium: Idaho Center

The **2009 Special Olympics World Winter Games** was held in the state of Idaho, USA from February 7 through February 13, 2009.

Nearly 2500 athletes from over 100 countries participated in the games. Dignitaries included actors, musicians, athletes and politicians from around the United States and the world. Vice President Joe Biden participated in figure skating[1], presented awards to athletes, and met athletes and their families at other events on Thursday, February 12. He further announced the appointment of Kareem Dale as special assistant to the president for disability policy. [2]

The following cities hosted the games:

- Boise
- McCall, ID
- Sun Valley

Venues

- Snowshoeing - McCall (Ponderosa State Park)
- Floor Hockey - Boise (Idaho Expo)
- Alpine Skiing - Boise (Bogus Basin Ski Resort)
- Figure Skating - Boise (Qwest Arena)
- Speed skating - Boise (Idaho Ice World)
- Cross-country Skiing - Sun Valley (Sun Valley Nordic Center)
- Snowboarding - Sun Valley (Dollar Mountain)

Websites (URLs online)

- Official Site
- Flame of Hope
- Morley the Mascot

References (URLs online)

- 1. "Vice President Joe Biden: 'This is a movement' for change". IdahoStatesman.com. 13 February 2009. Retrieved 2 September 2009.
- 2. http://www.idahostatesman.com/1266/story/666947.html "Vice President Joe Biden: 'This is a movement' for change", Idaho Statesman, 02/13/09

A hyperlinked version of this chapter is at http://booksllc.net?q=2009%5FSpecial% 5FOlympics%5FWorld%5FWinter%5FGames

9

2011 SPECIAL OLYMPICS WORLD SUMMER GAMES

13th Special Olympics World Summer Games

- Opening ceremony: 25 June 2011
- Closing ceremony: 4 July 2011

The **2011 Special Olympics World Summer Games** will be held during Summer 2011 in Athens, Greece.

Summer sports

- Aquatics
- Athletics (track and field)
- Badminton
- Basketball
- Bocce
- Bowling
- Cycling
- Equestrian

- Floor Hockey
- Football (Soccer)
- Golf
- Gymnastics
- Judo
- Powerlifting
- Roller Skating
- Sailing
- Softball
- Table Tennis
- Team Handball
- Tennis
- Volleyball
- Checkers

Possible inclusion

- Canoeing[1]

References (URLs online)

- 1. 25 August 2009 Canoeicf.com article in paddleability's inclusion into the 2011 Special Olympics following the success of the 2009 ICF Canoe Sprint World Championships. - accessed 1 September 2009.

Websites (URLs online)

- Special Olympics
- 2011 World Summer Games - official site

A hyperlinked version of this chapter is at http://booksllc.net?q=2011%5FSpecial%5FOlympics%5FWorld%5FSummer%5FGames

A VERY SPECIAL ACOUSTIC CHRISTMAS

A Very Special Acoustic Christmas

- Compilation album by A Very Special Christmas
- Released: October 21, 2003
- Genre: Christmas music
- Label: Lost Highway Records
- A Very Special Christmas chronology
- *A Very Special Christmas 5* (2001): *A Very Special Acoustic Christmas* (2003): *A Very Special Christmas 7* (2009)

A Very Special Acoustic Christmas is the sixth in a series of Christmas music-themed compilation albums produced to benefit the Special Olympics. The album was released in 2003 by Lost Highway Records. As opposed to earlier editions that contained a wide variety of musical styles, this version of A Very Special Christmas featured primarily Country and Bluegrass artists.

Track listing

- ○ "Silent Night" - Reba McEntire
- ○ "Frosty the Snowman" - Dan Tyminski
- ○ "Please Come Home for Christmas" - Willie Nelson
- ○ "Just Put a Ribbon in Your Hair" - Alan Jackson
- ○ "Only You Can Bring Me Cheer (Gentleman's Lady)" - Alison Krauss
- ○ "Even Santa Gets the Blues" - Marty Stuart
- ○ "Jingle Bells" - Earl Scruggs
- ○ "Christmas Is Near" - Ralph Stanley
- ○ "O Come All Ye Faithful" - Patty Loveless
- ○ "O Holy Night" - Wynonna
- ○ "Winter Wonderland" - Pat Green
- ○ "Let It Snow, Let It Snow, Let It Snow" - Sam Bush
- ○ "Away in a Manger" - Ricky Skaggs
- ○ "Christmas Time at Home" - Rhonda Vincent
- ○ "I'll Be Home For Christmas" - Tift Merritt
- ○ "Peace" - Norah Jones

Release history

Year: Label: Format: Catalog

- ○ 2003: Lost Highway: CD: 000103802

References (URLs online)

- ○ Album information from Special Olympics

A hyperlinked version of this chapter is at http://booksllc.net?q=A%5FVery%5FSpecial%5FAcoustic%5FChristmas

11

A VERY SPECIAL CHRISTMAS (ALBUM)

A Very Special Christmas

- o Compilation album by A Very Special Christmas
- o Released: 1987
- o Genre: Christmas music
- o Length: 51:11
- o Label: A&M Records
- o Producer: Jimmy Iovine
- o Professional reviews
- o   o Allmusic link
- o A Very Special Christmas chronology
- o : *A Very Special Christmas* (1987): *A Very Special Christmas 2* (1992)

A Very Special Christmas is the first in a series of Christmas-themed compilation albums produced to benefit Special Olympics. The album was released in 1987, and production was overseen by Jimmy Iovine for A&M Records. The album sold over 1 million copies and raised millions of dollars for the Special Olympics.[1]

The cover artwork was designed by Keith Haring.

Track listing

- ○ "Santa Claus Is Coming to Town" - The Pointer Sisters
- ○ "Winter Wonderland" - Eurythmics
- ○ "Do You Hear What I Hear?" - Whitney Houston
- ○ "Merry Christmas Baby" - Bruce Springsteen and the E Street Band
- ○ "Have Yourself a Merry Little Christmas" - The Pretenders
- ○ "I Saw Mommy Kissing Santa Claus" - John Cougar Mellencamp
- ○ "Gabriel's Message" - Sting
- ○ "Christmas in Hollis" - Run D.M.C.
- ○ "Christmas (Baby Please Come Home)" - U2
- ○ "Santa Baby" - Madonna
- ○ "The Little Drummer Boy" - Bob Seger & The Silver Bullet Band
- ○ "Run Rudolph Run" - Bryan Adams
- ○ "Back Door Santa" - Bon Jovi
- ○ "The Coventry Carol" - Alison Moyet
- ○ "Silent Night" - Stevie Nicks

- ○ On later pressings of the album, "Back Door Santa" was replaced with "I Wish Every Day Could Be Like Christmas", also by Bon Jovi.

References (URLs online)

- ○ 1. McGee, Matt (2008). *U2:A Diary*. Omnibus Press. pp. 111. ISBN 978-1-84772-108-2.

Websites (URLs online)

- ○ A Very Special Christmas at Amazon.com
- ○ Special Olympics: A Very Special Christmas

A hyperlinked version of this chapter is at http://booksllc.net?q=A%5FVery%5FSpecial%5FChristmas%5F%28album%29

12

A VERY SPECIAL CHRISTMAS (SERIES)

A Very Special Christmas is the title of an ongoing series of Christmas music compilation albums that benefit Special Olympics. It features songs performed by artists from a variety of genres, such as U2, Stevie Nicks, Bon Jovi, Madonna, No Doubt, Whitney Houston, Run D.M.C., Willie Nelson and Bruce Springsteen.

A Very Special Christmas was the brainchild of music producer Jimmy Iovine, who wanted to produce a Christmas album as a memorial to his father. The idea of the record benefiting Special Olympics was suggested by Iovine's wife Vicki, as she was a volunteer for the organization. Herb Alpert and Jerry Moss, the founders of A&M Records, along with Bobby Shriver, helped the Iovines realize the project. Since the release of the first album in 1987, the series has raised over $100 million for Special Olympics, more than any other benefit series. The album cover art is designed by artist Keith Haring.

A Very Special Christmas series

- A Very Special Christmas - 1987

- A Very Special Christmas 2 - 1992
- A Very Special Christmas 3 - 1997
- A Very Special Christmas Live - 1999
- A Very Special Christmas 5 - 2001
- A Very Special Acoustic Christmas - 2003
- A Very Special Christmas 7 - 2009

Jazz to the World and *World Christmas*

In 1995, the jazz-oriented *Jazz to the World* was released by Blue Note Records. The following year, *World Christmas*, which focused on diverse artists from around the globe, was released by Blue Note subsidiary Metro Blue Records. Although they are not part of the main *A Very Special Christmas* series, the proceeds from these albums also benefit Special Olympics.

Jazz to the World

- "Winter Wonderland" - Herb Alpert/Jeff Lorber
- "Baby, It's Cold Outside" - Lou Rawls/Dianne Reeves
- "It Came Upon the Midnight Clear" - Fourplay
- "Have Yourself a Merry Little Christmas" - Diana Krall
- "O Tannenbaum" - Stanley Clarke/George Duke/Everette Harp
- "Let It Snow" - Michael Franks/Carla Bley/Steve Swallow
- "The Christmas Waltz" - The Brecker Brothers/Steve Kahn
- "The Little Drummer Boy" - Cassandra Wilson
- "I'll Be Home for Christmas" - Herbie Hancock/Eliane Elias
- "O come, O come, Emmanuel" - John McLaughlin
- "Christmas Blues" - Holly Cole
- "Angels We Have Heard on High" - Steps Ahead
- "The Christmas Song" - Anita Baker
- "What Child Is This?" - Chick Corea
- "Winter Wonderland" - Dave Koz
- "Il Est Ne, Le Divin Enfant" - Dr. John

World Christmas

- "Angels We Have Heard on High/Les Anges Dans Nos Compagnes" - Papa Wemba/Mino Cinelu
- "We Three Kings" - Bob Berg/Jim Beard/Zakir Hussain/Mark Ledford
- "Go Tell It on the Mountain" - John Scofield/The Wild Magnolias
- "O Holy Night" (Zan Vevede) - Angélique Kidjo
- "Michaux Veillait/Santa Claus Is Coming to Town" - The Caribbean Jazz Project
- "Natal" - Cesária Évora
- "Ave Maria" - Deep Forest/Louka Kanza
- "We Wish You a Merry Christmas/Rumba Navidene" - Vocal Sampling
- "Boas Festas" - Gilberto Gil/Caetano Veloso/Eliane Elias
- "Cascabel/Jingle Bells" - Yomo Toro and the Boricua All Stars
- "The Twelve Days of Christmas" - Mino Cinelu/Dianne Reeves

- ○ "God Rest Ye Merry Gentlemen" - Joshua Redman/Marcus Miller/Lalah Hathaway
- ○ "Navidad" - Gipsy Kings

Websites (URLs online)

- ○ Special Olympics official website

A hyperlinked version of this chapter is at http://booksllc.net?q=A%5FVery%5FSpecial%5FChristmas%5F%28series%29

A VERY SPECIAL CHRISTMAS 2

A Very Special Christmas 2

- o Compilation album by A Very Special Christmas
- o Released: October 20, 1992
- o Genre: Christmas music
- o Length: 69:34
- o Label: A&M Records
- o Producer: Jimmy Iovine, Vicki Iovine, Robert Sargent Shriver
- o Professional reviews
- o   o Allmusic link
- o A Very Special Christmas chronology
- o *A Very Special Christmas* (1987): *A Very Special Christmas 2* (1992): *A Very Special Christmas 3* (1997)

A Very Special Christmas 2 is the second in a series of Christmas-themed compilation albums produced to benefit Special Olympics. The album was released on 20 October 1992, and production was overseen by Jimmy Iovine, Vicki Iovine and Robert Sargent Shriver for A&M Records.

Special Olympics.   **29**

Track listing

- o "Christmas All Over Again" - Tom Petty and the Heartbreakers
- o "Jingle Bell Rock" - Randy Travis
- o "The Christmas Song" - Luther Vandross
- o "Santa Claus Is Coming to Town" - Frank Sinatra/Cyndi Lauper
- o "The Birth of Christ" - Boyz II Men
- o "Please Come Home for Christmas" - Jon Bon Jovi
- o "What Christmas Means to Me" - Paul Young
- o "O Christmas Tree" - Aretha Franklin
- o "Rockin' Around the Christmas Tree" - Ronnie Spector/Darlene Love
- o "White Christmas" - Michael Bolton
- o "Christmas Is" - Run D.M.C.
- o "Christmas Time Again" - Extreme
- o "Merry Christmas Baby" - Bonnie Raitt and Charles Brown
- o "O Holy Night" - Tevin Campbell
- o "Sleigh Ride" - Debbie Gibson
- o "What Child Is This?" - Vanessa Williams
- o "Blue Christmas" - Ann & Nancy Wilson
- o "Silent Night" - Wilson Phillips
- o "I Believe in You" - Sinéad O'Connor

Websites (URLs online)

- o A Very Special Christmas 2 at Amazon.com
- o Special Olympics: A Very Special Christmas

A hyperlinked version of this chapter is at http://booksllc.net?q=A%5FVery%5FSpecial%5FChristmas%5F2

14

A VERY SPECIAL CHRISTMAS 3

A Very Special Christmas 3

- o Compilation album by A Very Special Christmas
- o Released: September 23, 1997
- o Genre: Christmas music
- o Length: 65:57
- o Label: A&M Records
- o Producer: Bobby Shriver, Al Cafaro, Linda Feder
- o Professional reviews
- o   o Allmusic link
- o A Very Special Christmas chronology
- o *A Very Special Christmas 2* (1992): *A Very Special Christmas 3* (1997): *A Very Special Christmas Live* (1999)

A Very Special Christmas 3 is the third in a series of Christmas-themed compilation albums produced to benefit Special Olympics. The album was released on 23 September 1997, and production was overseen by Bobby Shriver, Al Cafaro, and Linda Feder for A&M Records.

Track listing

- "I Saw Three Ships" - Sting
- "Christmastime" - The Smashing Pumpkins
- "Children, Go Where I Send Thee" - Natalie Merchant
- "Santa Baby" - Rev Run & the Christmas All Stars featuring Mase, Puff Daddy, Snoop Doggy Dogg, Salt N' Pepa, Onyx & Keith Murray
- "Oi to the World" - No Doubt
- "Blue Christmas" - Sheryl Crow
- "Christmas" - Blues Traveler
- "Oiche Chiun (Silent Night)" - Enya
- "The Christmas Song" - Hootie & the Blowfish
- "Ave Maria" - Chris Cornell with Eleven
- "Christmas in the City" - Mary J. Blige featuring Angie Martinez
- "Santa Claus Is Back in Town" - Jonny Lang
- "Christmas Song" - Dave Matthews & Tim Reynolds
- "Christmas Is Now Drawing Near At Hand" - Steve Winwood
- "O Holy Night" - Tracy Chapman
- "We Three Kings" - Patti Smith

Websites (URLs online)

- A Very Special Christmas 3 at Amazon.com
- A Very Special Christmas 3 at Discogs
- Special Olympics: A Very Special Christmas

References (URLs online)

- Chart at Allmusic

A hyperlinked version of this chapter is at http://booksllc.net?q=A%5FVery%5FSpecial%5FChristmas%5F3

A VERY SPECIAL CHRISTMAS 5

A Very Special Christmas 5

- o Compilation album by A Very Special Christmas
- o Released: October 30, 2001
- o Genre: Christmas music
- o Label: A&M Records/Interscope Records
- o Producer: Bobby Shriver, Jon Bon Jovi, Joel Gallen
- o Professional reviews
- o   o Allmusic link
- o A Very Special Christmas chronology
- o *A Very Special Christmas Live* (1999): *A Very Special Christmas 5* (2001): *A Very Special Acoustic Christmas* (2003)

A Very Special Christmas 5 is the fifth in a series of Christmas-themed compilation albums produced to benefit Special Olympics. Several of the album's tracks were recorded live in Washington, D.C. in December 2000 at a benefit concert hosted by then-President Bill Clinton and First Lady Hillary Rodham Clinton. The album was released on 30 October 2001, with production supervision by Bobby Shriver, Jon Bon Jovi, and Joel Gallen for A&M Records.

Track listing

- ○ "This Christmas (Hang All the Mistletoe)" - Macy Gray
- ○ "Little Drummer Boy/Hot Hot Hot" - Wyclef Jean
- ○ "Noel! Noel!" - Eve 6
- ○ "Blue Christmas" - Jon Bon Jovi
- ○ "Merry Christmas Baby" - Stevie Wonder & Wyclef Jean
- ○ "O Come All Ye Faithful" - City High
- ○ "Christmas Is the Time to Say I Love You" - SR-71
- ○ "Christmas Day" - Dido
- ○ "Run Rudolph Run" - Sheryl Crow
- ○ "Back Door Santa" - B.B. King & John Popper
- ○ "Little Red Rooster" - Tom Petty & the Heartbreakers
- ○ "Christmas Don't Be Late (Chipmunk Song)" - Powder
- ○ "Silent Night" - Stevie Nicks
- ○ "I Love You More" - Stevie Wonder & Kimberly Brewer
- ○ "White Christmas" - Darlene Love

Websites (URLs online)

- ○ A Very Special Christmas 5 at Amazon.com
- ○ Special Olympics: A Very Special Christmas

A hyperlinked version of this chapter is at http://booksllc.net?q=A%5FVery%5FSpecial%5FChristmas%5F5

A VERY SPECIAL CHRISTMAS 7

A Very Special Christmas 7

- o Compilation album by A Very Special Christmas
- o Released: Nov. 24th, 2009
- o Recorded: 2009
- o Genre: Christmas
- o A Very Special Christmas chronology
- o *A Very Special Acoustic Christmas* (2003): *A Very Special Christmas 7* (2009):

A Very Special Christmas 7 is a collection of Christmas songs covered by current artists. The compilation album is the 7th in the series of albums. Vol.7 was released on November 24, 2009 and proceeds from sales will benefit the Special Olympics.

Vol. 7 returns to the original format of including artists from a wide range of musical styles, including genres from reggae fusion (Sean Kingston) to country (Kellie Pickler).

Track listing

○ Have Yourself A Merry Little Christmas by Colbie Caillat
○ Let It Snow by Carter Twins
○ Rockin' Around The Christmas Tree by Miley Cyrus
○ Winter Wonderland by Vanessa Hudgens
○ Little Drummer Boy by Sean Kingston
○ The Christmas Song by Charice
○ Do You Hear What I Hear by Kristinia Debarge
○ Jingle Bell Rock by Mitchel Musso
○ Christmas (Baby Please Come Home) by Leighton Meester
○ Santa Baby by Kellie Pickler
○ Hark! The Herald Angels Sing by Carrie Underwood
○ Last Christmas by Ashley Tisdale
○ Silent Night by Gloriana

Websites (URLs online)

○ on AMAZON
○ Special Olympics Very Special Christmas website
○ Official website

A hyperlinked version of this chapter is at http://booksllc.net?q=A%5FVery%
5FSpecial%5FChristmas%5F7

A VERY SPECIAL CHRISTMAS LIVE

A Very Special Christmas Live

- o Live album by A Very Special Christmas
- o Released: October 19, 1999
- o Recorded: Washington, D.C., December 1998
- o Genre: Christmas music
- o Length: 38:25
- o Label: A&M Records/Interscope Records
- o Professional reviews
- o   o Allmusic link
- o A Very Special Christmas chronology
- o *A Very Special Christmas 3* (1997): *A Very Special Christmas Live* (1999): *A Very Special Christmas 5* (2001)

A Very Special Christmas Live is the fourth in a series of Christmas music-themed compilation albums produced to benefit Special Olympics. The album was recorded live in Washington, D.C. in December 1998 at a benefit party held by then-President Bill Clinton and First Lady Hillary Rodham Clinton to celebrate the thirtieth anniversary of the founding of Special Olympics. It was released on 19 October 1999, and production was overseen by Bobby Shriver for A&M Records.

Track listing

- o "Rockin' Around the Christmas Tree" Mary J. Blige and Sheryl Crow
- o "Christmas in Hollis" Run D.M.C.
- o "Please Come Home for Christmas" Jon Bon Jovi
- o "Christmas Blues" John Popper with Eric Clapton
- o "What Child Is This?" Vanessa Williams
- o "Christmas Tears" Eric Clapton
- o "O Holy Night" Tracy Chapman
- o "Give Me One Reason" Tracy Chapman and Eric Clapton
- o "Merry Christmas Baby" Sheryl Crow with Eric Clapton
- o "Christmas (Baby Please Come Home)" Jon Bon Jovi
- o "Santa Claus Is Coming to Town" Mary J. Blige, Jon Bon Jovi, Tracy Chapman, Eric Clapton, Sheryl Crow, John Popper, Run D.M.C., Vanessa Williams

Websites (URLs online)

- o A Very Special Christmas Live at Amazon.com

A hyperlinked version of this chapter is at http://booksllc.net?q=A%5FVery%5FSpecial%5FChristmas%5FLive

18

ANNE M. BURKE

Anne McGlone Burke, SMOM (born February 3, 1944) is an Illinois Supreme Court Justice for the First Judicial District (Cook County, Illinois)[1] and, along with other notables including Eunice Kennedy, is a founder of the Special Olympics.[2] Judge Burke was first appointed by the Illinois Supreme Court in 1995 and then was elected to the Appellate Court in 1996.

Biography

Burke was born and raised on Chicago's South Side, graduating from Maria High School. While raising her children, she returned to school and received a bachelor's degree from DePaul University in 1976 and a law degree from Chicago-Kent College of Law in 1983.

She was admitted to the Illinois bar and federal Northern District of Illinois in 1983, and the U.S. Court of Appeals for the 7th Circuit in 1985. She was certified for the Northern District's trial bar in 1987. The same year, Illinois Governor James Thompson appointed her a judge of the Illinois Court of Claims, and she was reappointed by

Governor Jim Edgar in 1991. Burke was the first woman to serve on the Illinois Court of Claims.

In April 1994, she was appointed special counsel to the Governor for Child Welfare Services. In August 1995, she was appointed to the Appellate Court, First District, and was subsequently elected to that office in 1996. Upon the retirement of Justice Mary Ann G. McMorrow in 2006, she was appointed to the Illinois Supreme Court. She was elected to a full 10-year term in November 2008.

Affiliations

She has also chaired the lay National Review Board of the U.S. Conference of Catholic Bishops which investigates accusations of clerical sexual abuse in the Roman Catholic church. She is a Dame of Malta.

Family

She is married to Alderman Edward M. Burke from the 14th Ward of the Chicago City Council and Chairman of the Committee on Finance.

The Burkes have four children, Jennifer, Edward Jr., Emmett and Sarah, and one grandchild, Kelley Anne. The Burkes are licensed, active foster parents.

Anne Burke has two brothers, Jack and George McGlone, and one sister, the late Patricia Cleary.

References (URLs online)

- ○ 1. Supreme Court of Illinois, "Justice Burke Bio", accessed 20 Sept. 2008.
- ○ 2. Kenidrigan & Hodkinson, "Special Olympics Celebrates 30 Years", accessed 20 Sept. 2008.

A hyperlinked version of this chapter is at http://booksllc.net?q=Anne%5FM%2E%5FBurke

ESTONIA AT THE SPECIAL OLYMPICS WORLD GAMES

Online image: Flag of Estonia

Estonia team have competed at the Special Olympics World Games since after regaining independence in 1991 and have won over 100 medals at the games.[1]

Medal tallies

Special Olympics World Summer Games

Event: Gold: Silver: Bronze: Total: Ranking: Athletes

- o 1991 Special Olympics World Summer Games: 2: 1: : : :
- o 1995 Special Olympics World Summer Games: : : : : :
- o 1999 Special Olympics World Summer Games: : : : : :
- o 2003 Special Olympics World Summer Games: 3: 1: 3: 7: : 7
- o 2007 Special Olympics World Summer Games: 4: 4: 5: 13: : 8
- o **Estonia Total**: : : : :

Best performances in bold.

Gold medalists

○ 2007 Special Olympics World Summer Games
  ○ Kalle Noorkõiv: Aquatics (swimming) Division M20 - Men's 100 metre freestyle 2.03,74
  ○ Anu Säär: Aquatics (swimming) Division F09 - Women's 50 metre freestyle 1.02,85
  ○ Ragne Kändla: Aquatics (swimming) Division F01 - Women's 100 metre freestyle 1.58,16
  ○ Viljar Koppel: Athletics/Track & Field Division M19 - Men's 400 metre run 1.12,57
○ 2003 Special Olympics World Summer Games
  ○ Riho Saar: Aquatics (swimming), Age Group: 16- 21, Division M35 - Men's 50 metre freestyle
  ○ Arvo Sõerd: Athletics/Track & Field - Men's 400 metre run
  ○ Estonian team (Gristel Markus, Arvo Sõerd, Angela Siim, Taivo Sõts): Athletics/Track & Field - 4x100 metre run
○ 1991 Special Olympics World Summer Games
  ○ Joel Zoova: Athletics/Track & Field

Silver medalists

○ 2007 Special Olympics World Summer Games
  ○ Viljar Koppel: Athletics/Track & Field Division M09 - Men's long jump 4.26
  ○ Raivo Laar: Athletics/Track & Field Division M07 - Men's 400 metre Run 1.01,92
  ○ Marge Vaino: Athletics/Track & Field Division F04 - Women's 800 metre run 2.48,72
  ○ Marge Vaino: Athletics/Track & Field Division F02 - Women's long jump 3.52
○ 2003 Special Olympics World Summer Games
  ○ Arvo Sõerd: Athletics/Track & Field, Age Group: 8- 11, Division M20 - Men's long jump
○ 1995 Special Olympics World Summer Games
  ○ Andrei Golovin: Powerlifting
○ 1991 Special Olympics World Summer Games
  ○ Arnold Oksmaa: Gymnastics
    ○ Estonian team (Arnold Oksmaa 2. place Sten Meriväli 4. place): Gymnastics

Bronze medalists

○ 2007 Special Olympics World Summer Games
  ○ Raivo Laar: Athletics/Track & Field Division M03 - Men's 1500 metre run 5.21,76
  ○ Jüri Kändla: Aquatics (swimming) Division M02 - Men's 50 metre freestyle 49,88
  ○ Kalle Noorkõiv: Aquatics (swimming) Division M17 - Men's 50 metre freestyle 43,50
  ○ Team Estonia (Jüri Kändla, Kalle Noorkõiv, Anu Säär, Ragne Kändla): Aquatics (swimming) Division M4 - 4X25 metre freestyle relay 1.26,78

- 2003 Special Olympics World Summer Games
  - Annika Holtsmann: Aquatics (swimming), Age Group: 16- 21, Division F10 - Women's 50 metre freestyle
  - Angela Siim: Athletics/Track & Field, Age Group: 16- 21, Division F01 - Women's 1500 metre run
  - Taivo Sõts: Athletics/Track & Field, Age Group: 16- 21, Division M01 - Men's shot put

Special Olympics World Winter Games

Event: Gold: Silver: Bronze: Total: Ranking: Athletes

- 1993 Special Olympics World Winter Games: 0: 0: 0: 0: :
- 1997 Special Olympics World Winter Games: 5: 7: 4: 16: : 8
- 2001 Special Olympics World Winter Games: 10: 4: 3: 17: : 8
- 2005 Special Olympics World Winter Games: 4: 3: 1: 8: : 8
- **Estonia Total**: : : : **51** (49[2]):

Best performances in bold.

Gold medalists

- 2005 Special Olympics World Winter Games
  - Allar Sonn: Cross country skiing - Men's 1 km freestyle
  - Arbo Skobiej: Cross country skiing - Men's 5 km individual
  - Enno Rakojed: Cross country skiing - Men's 5 km freestyle 20.34,50
  - Estonian team (Enno Rakojed, Arbo Skobiej, Raigo Moor, Gustav Rannamets): Cross country skiing - Men's 4x1 km freestyle 16.12,0
- 2001 Special Olympics World Winter Games
  - Jannes Aasorg, Gennadi Grudkin, Airet Lohu, Urmas Simus, Marina Västrik, Eda King, Eerika Sõrmus and Kadi Kurn.
- 1997 Special Olympics World Winter Games
  - Erki Elmik: Cross country skiing - Men's 3 km freestyle
  - Liina Vingel: Cross country skiing - Women's km freestyle
  - Thule Kariste
  - Rainer Danilov

Silver medalists

- 2005 Special Olympics World Winter Games
  - Sven Paulus: Cross country skiing - Men's 1 km freestyle
  - Gustav Rannamets: Cross country skiing - Men's 3 km freestyle 12.29,60
  - Raigo Moor: Cross country skiing - Men's 5 km freestyle 21.16,00
- 1997 Special Olympics World Winter Games
  - Anu Säär: Cross country skiing - Women's 1 km freestyle
  - Estonian team (Erki Elmik, Marek Sepp, Eiko Hallkivi): Cross country skiing - Men's 3x1 km freestyle

Bronze medalists

- o 2005 Special Olympics World Winter Games
  - o Enno Rakojed: Cross country skiing - Men's 3 km freestyle 13.22,70
- o 1997 Special Olympics World Winter Games
  - o Rene Ridal: Cross country skiing - Men's 1 km freestyle
  - o Marek Sepp: Cross country skiing - Men's 3 km freestyle

See also (online edition)

- o President and Honorary patron of the Special Olympics Estonia (Eesti Eriolümpia)
  - o Tõnu Karu 1989 1997
  - o Toomas Hendrik Ilves 1997 2004 (now Honorary President)
  - o Honorary patron since 2004: Jaak Jõerüüt
- o Estonia at the Olympics
- o Estonia at the Paralympics

Websites (URLs online)

- o Special Olympics
- o Special Olympics Estonia
- o Team Estonia at 2007 Special Olympics World Summer Games

A hyperlinked version of this chapter is at http://booksllc.net?q=Estonia%5Fat%5Fthe%5FSpecial%5FOlympics%5FWorld%5FGames

EUNICE KENNEDY SHRIVER

Eunice Kennedy Shriver

- ○ Zurab Tsereteli with Eunice Kennedy Shriver (right) (unknown date).
- ○ Born: Eunice Mary Kennedy July 10, 1921(1921-07-10) Brookline, Massachusetts, United States
- ○ Died: August 11, 2009 (aged 88) Hyannis, Massachusetts, United States
- ○ Resting place: St. Francis Xavier Roman Catholic Church parish cemetery Centerville, Massachusetts, United States[1]
- ○ *Alma mater*: Stanford University
- ○ Political party: Democratic
- ○ Religion: Roman Catholic
- ○ Spouse(s): Robert Sargent Shriver, Jr. (1953 2009, her death)
- ○ Children: Robert Sargent Shriver III Maria Owings Shriver Timothy Perry Shriver Mark Kennedy Shriver Anthony Paul Kennedy Shriver
- ○ Parents: Joseph P. Kennedy, Sr. Rose Kennedy (*née* Fitzgerald)
- ○ Relatives: *see Kennedy family*
- ○ **Website** eunicekennedyshriver.org

Eunice Kennedy Shriver DSG (July 10, 1921 August 11, 2009)[2] founded Camp Shriver, the precursor to the Special Olympics, in 1962. In 1968, she founded the Special Olympics.

She was a member of the Kennedy family and actively campaigned for her elder brother, U.S. President John F. Kennedy, during his successful 1960 U.S. presidential election. Her husband, Robert Sargent Shriver, Jr., is a former United States Ambassador to France, the founder of the Peace Corps, and was the Democratic vice-presidential candidate in the 1972 U.S. presidential election. Their daughter, Maria Shriver, is married to actor and current California Governor Arnold Schwarzenegger.

Personal life and early career

Born **Eunice Mary Kennedy** in Brookline, Massachusetts, she was the fifth of nine children of Joseph P. Kennedy, Sr. and Rose Fitzgerald.

She was educated at the Convent of the Sacred Heart, Roehampton, London, England; and Manhattanville College in Purchase, New York. After graduating from Stanford University with a Bachelor of Science degree in sociology in 1943,[3] she worked for the Special War Problems Division of the U.S. State Department. She eventually moved to the U.S. Justice Department as executive secretary for a project dealing with juvenile delinquency. She served as a social worker at the Federal Industrial Institution for Women for one year before moving to Chicago in 1951 to work with the House of the Good Shepherd women's shelter and the Chicago Juvenile Court.[4]

On May 23, 1953, she married Sargent Shriver in a Roman Catholic ceremony at Saint Patrick's Cathedral in New York City, New York.[5] Her husband served as the U.S. Ambassador to France from 1968 to 1970 and was the 1972 Democratic U.S. Vice Presidential candidate (with George McGovern as the candidate for U.S. President).[5] They had five children:

- o Robert Sargent Shriver III (born April 28, 1954)
- o Maria Owings Shriver (November 6, 1955)
- o Timothy Perry Shriver (August 29, 1959)
- o Mark Kennedy Shriver (February 17, 1964)
- o Anthony Paul Kennedy Shriver (July 20, 1965)

With her husband she had nineteen grandchildren, the second-most of any of the children of Joseph P. Kennedy, Sr. and Rose Kennedy. (Her brother U.S. Senator Robert F. Kennedy had eleven children who have produced thirty-two grandchildren.)

As executive vice president of the Joseph P. Kennedy, Jr. Foundation in the 1950s, she shifted the organization's focus from Catholic charities to research on the causes of people with intellectual disabilities and humane ways to treat it.[6] This interest eventually culminated in, among other things, the Special Olympics movement.

Upon the death of her sister, Rosemary Kennedy, on January 7, 2005, Shriver became the eldest of the four then-surviving children of Joseph and Rose Kennedy. Her sister, Patricia Kennedy Lawford, died on September 17, 2006, and her brother, U.S. Senator Edward M. Kennedy, on August 25, 2009, leaving her sister, former U.S. Ambassador to Ireland, Jean Kennedy Smith, as her only surviving sibling. [7]

Political career

Shriver actively campaigned for her elder brother, John, during his successful 1960 U.S. presidential election.

In 1968, she helped Burke nationalize the Special Olympics movement and is the only woman to have her portrait appear, during her lifetime, on a U.S. coin the 1995 commemorative Special Olympics silver dollar.

Although Shriver was a Democrat, she was a vocal supporter of the pro-life movement. In 1990, Shriver wrote a letter to *The New York Times* denouncing the misuse of a quotation by President Kennedy used out of context by a pro-choice group.[8] During Bill Clinton's 1992 Democratic U.S. presidential campaign, she was one of several prominent Democrats including Governor Robert P. Casey of Pennsylvania, and Bishop Austin Vaughan of New York who signed a letter to *The New York Times* protesting the Democratic Party's pro-choice plank in its platform. Shriver was a supporter of several pro-life organizations: Feminists for Life of America,[9] the Susan B. Anthony List,[10] and Democrats for Life of America.

A life-long Democrat, she supported her Republican son-in-law Schwarzenegger's successful 2003 Governor of California election.

On January 28, 2008, Shriver was present at American University in Washington, D.C., when her brother, U.S. Senator Edward M. Kennedy, announced his endorsement of Barack Obama's 2008 Democratic U.S. presidential campaign.[11]

Charity work and awards

See also: List of Presidential Medal of Freedom recipients

Online image: In 2008, the National Institute of Child Health and Human Development was renamed in honor of Eunice Kennedy Shriver.

A longtime advocate for children's health and disability issues, Shriver was a key founder of the National Institute of Child Health and Human Development (NICHD), a part of the National Institutes of Health, in 1962, and has also helped to establish numerous other health-care facilities and support networks throughout the country.

In 1982, Shriver founded the **Eunice Kennedy Shriver National Center for Community of Caring** at University of Utah, Salt Lake City. The Community is a *"grades K-12, whole school, comprehensive character education program with a focus on disabilities... adopted by almost 1,200 schools nationwide and in Canada."*[12]

She was awarded the nation's highest civilian award, the (U.S.) Presidential Medal of Freedom, in 1984 by U.S. President Ronald Reagan, because of her work on behalf of those with mental retardation.[13]

For her work in nationalizing the Special Olympics, Shriver received the Civitan International World Citizenship Award.[14] Her advocacy on this issue has also earned her other awards and recognitions, including honorary degrees from numerous universities.[15][16] She is the second American and only woman to appears on a US coin while still living. Her portrait is on the obverse of the 1995 commemorative silver dollar honoring the Special Olympics. On the reverse is the quotation, "As we hope for the best in them, hope is reborn in us."

Shriver received the 2002 Theodore Roosevelt Award (the Teddy),[17] an annual award given by the National Collegiate Athletic Association to a graduate from an NCAA member institution who earned a varsity letter in college for participation in intercollegiate athletics, and who ultimately became a distinguished citizen of national reputation based on outstanding life accomplishment.

In addition to the Teddy recognition, she was selected in 2006 as part of the NCAA Centennial celebration as one of the 100 most-influential individuals in its first century; she was listed ninth.[17]

Online image: Rare Halo Display: Portrait of Eunice Kennedy Shriver, *David Lenz, 2009 / National Portrait Gallery, Smithsonian Institution; commissioned as part of the First Prize, Outwin Boochever Portrait Competition 2006.*

In 2006 she received a papal knighthood from Pope Benedict XVI being named a Dame of the Order of St. Gregory the Great. Her mother had been created a papal countess in 1950 by Pope Pius XII.

In 2008, the U.S. Congress changed the NICHD s name to the *Eunice Kennedy Shriver* National Institute of Child Health and Human Development. In December 2008, Sports Illustrated named her the first recipient of Sportsman of the Year Legacy Award.[18]

On May 9, 2009, the Smithsonian Institution's National Portrait Gallery (NPG) in Washington, D.C., unveiled an historic portrait of her, the first portrait the NPG has ever commissioned of an individual who had not served as a U.S. President or First Lady. The portrait depicts her with four Special Olympics athletes (including Loretta Claiborne) and one Best Buddies participant. It was painted by David Lenz, the winner of the Outwin Boochever Portrait Competition in 2006. As part of the Portrait Competition prize, the NPG commissioned a work from the winning artist to depict a living subject for the collection. Lenz, whose son, Sam, has Down syndrome and is an enthusiastic Special Olympics athlete, was inspired by Shriver s dedication to working with people with intellectual disabilities.

Shriver became involved with Dorothy Hamill's special skating program in the Special Olympics after Hamill's Olympics Games ice-skating win.

Later years and death

Shriver, who was believed to have suffered from Addison's disease,[19] suffered a stroke and a broken hip in 2005, and on November 18, 2007, she was admitted to Massachusetts General Hospital in Boston, where she spent several weeks.[20][21]

On August 7, 2009, she was admitted to Cape Cod Hospital in Hyannis, with an undisclosed ailment.[22]

On August 10 her relatives were called to the hospital.[23] Early the following morning, Shriver died at the hospital; she was 88 years old.[2][24] No other Kennedy, with the exception of her mother, Rose, has, to date, lived longer.

Shriver's family issued a statement upon her death, reading in part

"Inspired by her love of God, her devotion to her family, and her relentless belief in the dignity and worth of every human life, she worked without ceasing searching, pushing, demanding, hoping for change. She was a living prayer, a living advocate, a living center of power. She set out to change the world and to change us, and she did that and more. She founded the movement that became Special Olympics, the largest movement for acceptance and inclusion for people with intellectual disabilities in the history of the world. Her work transformed the lives of hundreds of millions of people across the globe, and they in turn are her living legacy."[25]

Funeral and burial

On August 14, 2009, an invitation-only Requiem Mass was celebrated for Shriver at St. Francis Xavier Roman Catholic Church in Hyannis. Following the Requiem Mass, she was buried at the St. Francis Xavier parish cemetery in nearby Centerville.[1] Pope Benedict XVI sent a letter of condolence to her family.[26] Because of his ill health, her brother Ted couldn't attend the funeral,[27] and their sister, Jean Smith (now the sole surviving child of Joseph and Rose Kennedy), stayed with him. He died two weeks later.[27][7]

See also (online edition)

- Kennedy family
- National Institute of Child Health and Human Development
- Special Olympics

References (URLs online)

- 1. Staff writer (August 14, 2009). "Special Olympians, Family Celebrate Eunice Kennedy Shriver". *The Associated Press* (at WJAR television's website turnto10.com). Retrieved August 16, 2000.
- 2. Grinberg, Emanuella (undated). "Eunice Kennedy Shriver dies". Edition.cnn.com. Retrieved August 11, 2009.
- 3. Smith, J.Y. (August 11, 2009). "Eunice Kennedy Shriver, Founder of Special Olympics, Dies at 88" *The Washington Post.* Retrieved August 11, 2009.
- 4. Baranauckas, Carla (August 12, 2009). "Eunice Shriver, Founder of Special Olympics, Dies". *The New York Times.* (website registration required)
- 5. Archives. R(obert) "Sargent Shriver: An Inventory of His Personal Papers, 1948 1976, Papers (#214) J" John F. Kennedy Presidential Library & Museum, John F. Kennedy Library National Archives and Records Administration
- 6. "Eunice Kennedy Shriver, Special Olympics Founder, Dies at 88". washington-post.com. Retrieved 2010-03-02.
- 7. Staff writer. "Ted Kennedy Dies of Brain Cancer at Age 77 'Liberal Lion' of the Senate Led Storied Political Family After Deaths of President John F. Kennedy, Sen. Robert F. Kennedy". *ABC News.* Retrieved August 26, 2009.
- 8. Biofiles: Eunice Kennedy Shriver [1]. Retrieved August 11, 2009.
- 9. Shriver, Eunice Kennedy, "Remarkable Pro-Life Women" (PDF format) *The American Feminist, The Quarterly Magazine of Feminists for Life of America*, Vol. 5, No. 4, Winter 1998 1999, p. 18. Accessed May 28, 2008.
- 10. Susan B. Anthony List, Notable Names Database. Accessed May 28, 2008.
- 11. Alexander, Amy, "A Torch Passed", *The Nation*, January 28, 2008. Retrieved August 11, 2009.
- 12. "About Community of Caring". Eunice Kennedy Shriver National Center for Community of Caring. Undated. Retrieved August 14, 2009.
- 13. "Remarks at the Presentation Ceremony for the Presidential Medal of Freedom", Archives Ronald Reagan Presidential Library, administered by the National Archives and Records Administration. March 26, 1984. Accessed May 28, 2008.
- 14. Armbrester, Margaret E. (1992). *The Civitan Story.* Birmingham, AL: Ebsco Media. p. 95.
- 15. "Eunice Kennedy Shriver Doctor of Public Service" The Shriver Center, The University of Maryland, Baltimore County. Accessed May 28, 2008.
- 16. "Eunice Kennedy Shriver". *Special Olympics.* archive.org. Archived from the original on 2008-01-28. Retrieved August 12, 2009.
- 17. Staff writer (August 11, 2009). "2002 Teddy winner Shriver dies at 88". *NCAA News* (at the National Collegiate Athletic Association). Retrieved August 15, 2009.
- 18. Eunice Kennedy Shriver's legacy lives on with Special Olympics
- 19. Dallek, Robert (2003). *An Unfinished Life: John F. Kennedy, 1917 1963.* London: Penguin Books. pp. 105, 731. ISBN 978-0141015354.
- 20. "Eunice Kennedy Shriver Hospitalized". Associated Press. washingtonpost.com. November 25, 2007. Retrieved 2009-08-12.

o 21. Beggy, Carol and Mark Shanahan, "She's loyal to father's 'Ideal'", *The Boston Globe*, January 14, 2008. Retrieved August 11, 2009.
o 22. McGreevy, Patrick. "Schwarzenegger, Maria Shriver at Eunice Shriver's bedside", Los Angeles Times. August 7, 2009. Retrieved August 7, 2009.
o 23. Staff writer (August 11, 2009). "Eunice Kennedy Shriver's relatives called to hospital". CNN.com. Retrieved August 11, 2009.
o 24. Allen, Mike (August 11, 2009). "Eunice Kennedy Shriver dies". Politico.Com. Retrieved August 11, 2009.
o 25. "Statement from The Shriver Family". Eunice Kennedy Shriver's website. 2009-08-11. Retrieved 2009-08-11.
o 26. "Pope's Letter to Kennedy-Shriver Family". Retrieved 2009-08-20.
o 27. McMullen, Troy (August 26, 2009). "The Last Kennedy Death of Ted Kennedy Leaves One Surviving Child of Joseph and Rose Kennedy". *ABC News*. Retrieved August 26, 2009.

Websites (URLs online)

o eunicekennedyshriver.org, Shriver's official website
o "Statement from The Shriver Family", (August 11, 2009) on Shriver's official website
o Shriver, Maria (August 14, 2009). Transcript. "Maria Shriver's Eulogy of Her Mother", *The Boston Globe*. Accessed August 31, 2009.
o "Statement from the President on the Passing Of Eunice Kennedy Shriver", (August 11, 2009) on the White House's website
o Staff writer (undated). "Eunice Kennedy Shriver", obituary by *The Associated Press* (at *The Boston Globe*)
o Staff writer (August 11, 2009). "Eunice Kennedy Shriver", obituary at *The Daily Telegraph*
o "Special Olympians, Family Celebrate Eunice Kennedy Shriver", article on funeral and burial by *The Associated Press* (at WJAR television's website turnto10.com)
o Eunice Kennedy Shriver at the Internet Movie Database
o specialolympics.org, Special Olympics's official website
o communityofcaring.org, Eunice Kennedy Shriver National Center for Community of Caring's official website
o Shapiro, Joseph, Eunice Kennedy Shriver's Olympic Legacy, (April 5, 2007) *Morning Edition* on National Public Radio's website (includes podcast as well as text)
o Coin of the Month, U.S. Mint "Coin of the Month" page (geared for children) on the 1995 Special Olympics Commemorative Silver Dollar
o Eunice Kennedy Shriver at Find a Grave

Awards and achievements

o Preceded by **William Cohen: Theodore Roosevelt Award (NCAA) 2002**: Succeeded by **Donna de Varona**

A hyperlinked version of this chapter is at http://booksllc.net?q=Eunice%5FKennedy%5FShriver

21

FLAME OF HOPE

1. The **Flame of Hope** is a flame that was lit in 1989 as a tribute to Dr. Frederick Banting, who in 1922 discovered insulin, and all the people that have lost their lives to diabetes. The flame will remain lit until there is a cure for diabetes. The flame is located at Sir Fredrick Banting Square in London, Ontario, Canada.

Source: *Canada: A Nation Unfolding*

2. The **Flame of Hope** is a symbol of the Special Olympics. Used much in the same spirit as the Olympic Flame at the Olympic Games, the Flame of Hope is lit during a special traditional ceremony in Athens, Greece in the months running up to the Special Olympics World Games. It is then relayed on foot by Special Olympics athletes and members of law enforcement agencies from around the world; this is the culmination of the Law Enforcement Torch Run program, the main fundraising vehicle for Special Olympics.

At the end of its tour, the Flame is used to light a specially made beacon in the stadium which is to be the central location for those World Games.

See also (online edition)

- ○ Olympic Flame
- ○ Special Olympics
- ○ Olympic Games
- ○ Paralympics

A hyperlinked version of this chapter is at http://booksllc.net?q=Flame%5Fof%5FHope

22

HEALTHY ATHLETES

Healthy Athletes is an initiative run by the Special Olympics that offers athletes access to free health screenings and health information during local and international competitions. Health-care volunteers are present in 100 different countries and help people with intellectual disabilities receive adequate health care.

References (URLs online)

External Link

    ◦ Special Olympics

A hyperlinked version of this chapter is at http://booksllc.net?q=Healthy%5FAthletes

23

LAW ENFORCEMENT TORCH RUN

The **Law Enforcement Torch Run** Campaign to benefit the Special Olympics began in 1981 in Wichita, Kansas and is the largest grass-roots fundraising movement for the Special Olympics.

The Law Enforcement Torch Run, or LETR as it is commonly abbreviated, is run by Police Officers, Sheriff's Deputies, support staff, police volunteers and other law enforcement professionals from around the world.

Currently, close to 90,000 police professionals in over 35 countries participate in this worldwide effort to raise money and awareness for Special Olympics. Recently, the LETR has grown as a movement in several Latin American countries and is spreading to China.

Similar in many ways to the Olympic Torch Relay, the Law Enforcement Torch Run consists of scheduled relay events, usually held in conjunction and coordination with Special Olympics functions (like the Special Olympics Summer and Winter Games).

While carrying the flame, officers and athletes are referred to as "Guardians of the Flame".

To the left: Tip-a-cop, where local LEO's pair up with a restaurant to raise funds for special Olympics. Officers and Deputies will serve food and bus tables in uniform. Patrons will then give a donation to Special Olympics. The restaurant will also give a portion of the days take to the fund. Note this is a a Claim Jumper Restaurant, a chain that has chosen to support "Tip a Cop".

In the broader sense, the LETR is used to define all of the special events, and fundraising activities that law enforcement conducts to contribute to this campaign. This includes (but isn't limited to), Tip-a-Cop events, Car Washes, Polar Bear Plunges, Roof Sits, Motorcycle Runs, Online Fundraising, T-shirt and Hat sales, Media Events, and more.

Every two years, the Special Olympics World Games are held. This brings about a special torch run called the "Final Leg Run." During a final leg run, law enforcement, together with Special Olympic athletes run the Flame of Hope together throughout the host country for the games, spreading awareness for Special Olympics. This culminates with the lighting of the cauldron for the flame of hope at the opening ceremonies for the Special Olympics World Games. In 2007, the Summer World games will be held in Shanghai, China.

Every year, members of the LETR converge at the International LETR conference to exchange ideas, and network about Special Olympics awareness and fundraising techniques. In 2007, this conference will be held in Oklahoma.

Participants in the LETR help spread the word about the benefits of Special Olympics and how the program helps define the brave participants of these programs as athletes, and not define them by their disabilities.

Online image: LETR Torch runners display the Flame of Hope at Niagara Falls, Canada Nov. '06.

Online image: Washington Special Olympic Athletes and Redmond Police Officer at a fundraising & awareness event

Online image: A tip-a-cop event to benefit Special Olympics.

Online image: Officers go up on a rooftop of a local grocery store to raise money and awareness for Special Olympics.

   o Online image: Police Officers serve meals during a fundraising event.

See also (online edition)

- ○ Special Olympics World Games
- ○ Flame of Hope
- ○ Olympic Games

Websites (URLs online)

- ○ Special Olympics LETR Parent Website
- ○ 2007 World Games Official Website
- ○ Special Olympics Washington
- ○ Special Olympics Missouri Torch Run Information Page

A hyperlinked version of this chapter is at http://booksllc.net?q=Law%
5FEnforcement%5FTorch%5FRun

24

MEXICO AT THE SPECIAL OLYMPICS WORLD GAMES

Online image: Flag of Mexico

México has competed at the Special Olympics World Games 11 times.

Medal tallies

Special Olympics World Winter Games

Event: Gold: Silver: Bronze: Total: Ranking: Athletes

- 2009 Special Olympics World Winter Games: 1: 0: 2: 3: : 24
- *'Mexico Total* : : : : ':

Gold medalists

- 2009 Special Olympics World Winter Games
  - José Visiconty: Figure Skating Men's Singles Division 6

Silver medalists

Bronze medalists

- ○ 2009 Special Olympics World Winter Games
  - ○ Brenda Monreal and José Visiconty: Figure Skating Pairs Division 1
  - ○ Juan Ruiz: Figure Skating Men's Singles Division 6

Other Results

- ○ 2009 Special Olympics World Winter Games
  - ○ 4th: Mexican mixed Floor hockey team: Floor Hockey Mixed Competition Division I - Lost to Spain for 3rd place
    - ○ *Team members: Lilia Aguilar, Luis Baca, Saúl Campos, Juan Carrillo, Jesús García, Loreto López, Roberto Manzanares, Armando Murillo, Ever Ochoa, Angel Ortiz, Ever Ortiz, Hector Pacheco, Rosaura Reyes, Luz Rico, Beatriz Rivera and Jorge Sandoval.*
  - ○ 4th: Tomás Arenazas: Figure Skating Men's Singles Division 5
  - ○ 4th: Brenda Monreal: Figure Skating Women's Singles Division 1
  - ○ 6th: Alonso Flores: Figure Skating Men's Singles Division 6
  - ○ 6th: Rosa María Rodríguez: Figure Skating Women's Singles Division 2
  - ○ 7th: Jenny Arcos: Figure Skating Women's Singles Division 3
  - ○ 7th: Karen Borges: Figure Skating Women's Singles Division 1

See also (online edition)

- ○ Mexico at the Olympics
- ○ Mexico at the Paralympics

Websites (URLs online)

- ○ Special Olympics
- ○ Olimpiadas Especiales México
- ○ 2009 World Winter Games Website

A hyperlinked version of this chapter is at http://booksllc.net?q=Mexico%5Fat%5Fthe%5FSpecial%5FOlympics%5FWorld%5FGames

25

SARGENT SHRIVER

Robert Sargent Shriver

- o 21st United States Ambassador to France
- o **In office** April 22, 1968 March 25, 1970
- o President: Lyndon B. Johnson Richard Nixon
- o Preceded by: Charles E. Bohlen
- o Succeeded by: Arthur K. Watson
- o 1st Director of the Peace Corps
- o **In office** March 22, 1961 February 28, 1966[1]
- o President: John F. Kennedy Lyndon B. Johnson
- o Preceded by: (*None*)
- o Succeeded by: Jack Vaughn
- o 1st Director of the Office of Economic Opportunity
- o **In office** 1965 1968
- o President: Lyndon B. Johnson
- o Preceded by: (*None*)
- o Succeeded by: Bertrand Harding
- o Born: November 9, 1915 (1915-11-09) Westminster, Maryland
- o Political party: Democratic

- Spouse(s): Eunice Kennedy Shriver (1953 2009, her death)
- Children: Robert Sargent Shriver III Maria Owings Shriver Timothy Perry Shriver Mark Kennedy Shriver Anthony Paul Kennedy Shriver
- Alma mater: Yale University Yale Law School
- Profession: Attorney
- Religion: Roman Catholic
- Signature:
- **Military service**
- Allegiance: United States of America
- Service/branch: United States Navy
- Years of service: 1941 1945
- Rank: Lieutenant
- Battles/wars: World War II
- Awards: World War II Victory Medal, Purple Heart, Asiatic-Pacific Campaign Medal[2]

Robert Sargent Shriver, Jr. (born November 9, 1915) is an American Democratic politician and activist. Known as "Sargent", Shriver is best known as part of the Kennedy family, the driving force behind the creation of the Peace Corps, and the Democratic Party's replacement candidate for U.S. vice president having replaced nominee Thomas Eagleton, who resigned from the ticket during the 1972 U.S. presidential election. Upon the death of Jacqueline Kennedy Onassis, Shriver is one of only four living spouses (along with Joan Kennedy, Vicki Kennedy, and Ethel Kennedy) of the children of Joseph P. Kennedy and Rose Kennedy.

Early life and career

Shriver was born in Westminster, Maryland to Robert Sargent Shriver, Sr. and his wife Hilda Shriver. Of German ancestry, the Shriver family is descended from David Shriver, who signed the Maryland Constitution and Bill of Rights at Maryland's Constitutional Convention of 1776.[3] He spent his high school years at the Canterbury School in New Milford, Connecticut, which he attended on a full scholarship. After graduating, Shriver spent the summer in Germany as part of the Experiment in International Living, returning in the fall of 1934 to begin college at Yale University. He received his bachelor's degree in 1938 from Yale University, where he was a member of the Delta Kappa Epsilon fraternity (Phi chapter) and Scroll and Key Society. He was Chairman of the *Yale Daily News*. Shriver went on to attend Yale Law School, earning an LL.B. degree in 1941.

An early opponent of American involvement in World War II, Shriver was a founding member of America First, an organization that tried to keep America out of the war. Still, Shriver volunteered for the United States Navy, saying he had a duty to serve his country even if he disagreed with its policies. He spent five years in active duty, rising to the rank of lieutenant. Shriver ultimately came to believe in the justness of American involvement in the war and retracted his early opposition.

Shriver's involvement with the Kennedy family began when family patriarch Joseph Kennedy, Sr. hired him to manage the Merchandise Mart, part of Kennedy's business empire, in Chicago, Illinois.

At the age of nearly 38 and after a seven-year courtship, Shriver married Eunice Kennedy, a sister of then-Senator John F. Kennedy, on May 23, 1953 at St. Patrick's Cathedral in New York City.[4] They had five children: Robert Sargent Shriver III (born April 28, 1954), Maria Owings Shriver (born November 6, 1955), Timothy Perry Shriver (born August 29, 1959), Mark Kennedy Shriver (born February 17, 1964), and Anthony Paul Kennedy Shriver (born July 20, 1965).

Shriver is admitted to practice law in the District of Columbia, Illinois, New York, and at the U.S. Supreme Court.[5]

A devout Catholic, Shriver attends daily Mass and always carries a rosary of well-worn wooden beads.[6]

Political career

John F. Kennedy

When John F. Kennedy ran for president, Shriver worked as a political and organization coordinator in the Wisconsin and West Virginia primaries. During Kennedy's presidential term, Shriver served as the first director of the Peace Corps.

Lyndon B. Johnson

After Kennedy's assassination, Shriver continued to serve as Director of the Peace Corps and served as Special Assistant to President Johnson. Under Johnson, he created the Office of Economic Opportunity with William B. Mullins and served as the first Director.[7]

Political activism

Shriver founded numerous social programs and organizations, including Head Start, VISTA, Job Corps, Community Action, Upward Bound, Foster Grandparents, Special Olympics, Legal Services, the National Clearinghouse for Legal Services (now the Shriver Center), Indian and Migrant Opportunities and Neighborhood Health Services, and directed the Peace Corps. Shriver also ran the War on Poverty during Johnson's tenure as president. He was such an effective leader, that *Job Corps* and *Adams and Associates* dedicated a Center to his name in 1999. The Job Corps Center (**Shriver Job Corps**) is located in Devens, Massachusetts.

Ambassador to France

Shriver served as U.S. ambassador to France from 1968 to 1970, becoming a quasi-celebrity among the French for bringing what *Time magazine* called "a rare and welcome panache" to the normally sedate world of international diplomacy.

Vice Presidential candidate

Online image: Shriver and JFK

Shriver returned to elective politics in 1972, when George McGovern chose him as his Vice Presidential running mate after McGovern's first pick, Thomas Eagleton, resigned from the Democratic ticket following revelations of past mental health treatments. The McGovern-Shriver ticket lost to Republican incumbents Richard Nixon and Spiro Agnew. He remains to date the most recent pro-life candidate to have been in a Democratic Party presidential ticket.

Shriver sought the Democratic nomination for President in 1976. His candidacy was short and he returned to private life.[8]

Life after politics

He was associated with the Fried, Frank, Harris, Shriver & Jacobson law firm in the Washington, D.C., where he specialized in international law and foreign affairs, beginning in 1971.[5] He retired as partner in 1986 and was then named of counsel to the firm.[9]

In 1981, Shriver was appointed to the Rockefeller University Council, an organization devoted exclusively to research and graduate education in the biomedical and related sciences.

In 1984, he was elected President of Special Olympics by the Board of Directors; as President, he directed the operation and international development of sports programs around the world. Six years later, in 1990, he was appointed Chairman of the Board of Special Olympics.

He was an investor in the Baltimore Orioles along with his eldest son Bobby Shriver, Eli Jacobs and Larry Lucchino from 1989[10] to 1993.

Shriver was diagnosed with Alzheimer's disease in 2003. In 2004 his daughter, Maria, published a children's book, *What's Happening to Grandpa?*, to help explain Alzheimer's to children. The book gives suggestions on how to help and to show love to an elderly person with the disease.[11] In July 2007, Shriver's son-in-law, California Governor Arnold Schwarzenegger, speaking in favor of stem-cell research, said that Shriver's Alzheimer's disease had advanced to the point that "Today, he does not even recognize his wife."[12]

On August 11, 2009, Shriver's wife of 56 years, Eunice Kennedy Shriver, died at the age of 88. He attended his wife's wake and funeral mass in Centerville and Hyannis, Massachusetts.

Two weeks later, on August 29, 2009, he attended the funeral of his brother-in-law, Edward Kennedy in Boston, Massachusetts.

Legacy

In 1993, Shriver received the Franklin D. Roosevelt Freedom From Want Award. On August 8, 1994, Shriver received the Presidential Medal of Freedom, the United States' highest civilian honor, from President Bill Clinton.[9]

The National Clearinghouse for Legal Services (renamed the National Center on Poverty Law in 1995) was re-named the Shriver Center in 2002 and each year awards a Sargent Shriver Award for Equal Justice. [1]

Sargent Shriver Elementary School, located in Silver Spring, Maryland, is named after Shriver.[13][14][15]

In January 2008, a documentary film about Shriver aired on PBS, titled *American Idealist: The Story of Sargent Shriver.* [2]

Electoral history

United States presidential election, 1972

- Richard Nixon/Spiro Agnew (R) (inc.) - 47,168,710 (60.7%) and 520 electoral votes (49 states carried)
- George McGovern/Sargent Shriver (D) - 29,173,222 (37.5) and 17 electoral votes (1 state and D.C. carried)
- John Hospers/Theodora Nathan (Libertarian) - 3,674 (0.00%) and 1 electoral votes (Republican faithless elector)
- John G. Schmitz/Thomas J. Anderson (AI) - 1,100,868 (1.4%) and 0 electoral votes
- Linda Jenness/Andrew Pulley (Socialist Workers) - 83,380 (0.1%)
- Benjamin Spock/Julius Hobson (People's) - 78,759 (0.1%)

1976 Democratic presidential primaries[16]

- Jimmy Carter - 6,235,609 (39.27%)
- Jerry Brown - 2,449,374 (15.43%)
- George Wallace - 1,955,388 (12.31%)
- Mo Udall - 1,611,754 (10.15%)
- Henry M. Jackson - 1,134,375 (7.14%)
- Frank Church - 830,818 (5.23%)
- Robert Byrd - 340,309 (2.14%)

- ○ Sargent Shriver - 304,399 (1.92%)
- ○ Unpledged - 283,437 (1.79%)
- ○ Ellen McCormack - 238,027 (1.50%)
- ○ Fred R. Harris - 234,568 (1.48%)
- ○ Milton Shapp - 88,254 (0.56%)
- ○ Birch Bayh - 86,438 (0.54%)
- ○ Hubert Humphrey - 61,992 (0.39%)
- ○ Ted Kennedy - 19,805 (0.13%)
- ○ Lloyd Bentsen - 4,046 (0.03%)
- ○ Terry Sanford - 404 (0.00%)

See also (online edition)

- ○ List of United States political appointments that crossed party lines

References (URLs online)

- ○ 1. Past Directors.
- ○ 2. "A Muscular Idealism - New York Times". *The New York Times*. 2004-04-23. Retrieved 2008-12-05.
- ○ 3. "The New Nominee No Longer Half a Kennedy - TIME". Time Magazine. 1972-08-14. Retrieved 2008-09-27.
- ○ 4. R(obert) Sargent Shriver: Papers (#214) - John F. Kennedy Presidential Library & Museum
- ○ 5. "Sargent Shriver". Fried, Frank, Harris, Shriver & Jacobson LLP. Retrieved 2008-06-07.
- ○ 6. ""Sargent Shriver and the politics of life". National Catholic Reporter. 2002-08-30.
- ○ 7. W. B. Mullins, 52, A Founding Official Of the Peace Corps - New York Times
- ○ 8. "JFK Presidential Library Opens Sargent Shriver Collection". John F. Kennedy Presidential Library & Museum. 2005-02-01. Retrieved 2008-06-07.
- ○ 9. "Presidential Medal of Freedom Recipient Sargent R. Shriver". 1994-08-08. Retrieved 2008-06-08.
- ○ 10. Hyman, Mark S. "Orioles are sold: $70 million; Buyers say team will stay," *The Baltimore Sun*, December 7, 1988
- ○ 11. Shriver, Maria (April 28, 2004). *What's Happening to Grandpa?*. Little, Brown Young Readers. ISBN 978-0316001014.
- ○ 12. Benzie, Robert; Ferguson, Rob (May 31, 2007). "Terminator gunning to save lives; California governor, McGuinty sign stem-cell research deal in bid to 'cure a lot' of illnesses". *Toronto Star*. Retrieved 2008-06-07.
- ○ 13. Hands-on lessons for Shriver students
- ○ 14. New school year, new elementary school
- ○ 15. August 29: Sargent Shriver's Family Visits the New Shriver ES
- ○ 16. Our Campaigns - US President - D Primaries Race - Feb 01, 1976

Portrayals in film

The film *Too Young the Hero* (1988), about the life of Calvin Graham, features a scene during World War II in which Graham (played by Rick Schroder) meets Shriver (played by Carl Meuller).

The film *W.* (2008), about the life of George W. Bush, features Matt Sigloch as Shriver.

Further reading

- ○ Clinton, Bill (2004). *My Life*. New York: Knopf. ISBN 0091795273.
- ○ Stossel, Scott (2004). *Sarge: The Life and Times of Sargent Shriver*. Washington, D.C.: Smithsonian Books.

Websites (URLs online)

- ○ Biography at the Sargent Shriver Peace Institute
- ○ Biography at the Shriver Center
- ○ Peace Corps biography
- ○ Listing at Fried, Frank, Harris, Shriver & Jacobson Law Firm
- ○ American Idealist Movie, PBS
- ○ Ancestor David Shriver
- ○ Sargent Shriver National Center on Poverty Law

Government offices

- ○ Preceded by **none**: **Director of the Peace Corps** 1961 1966: Succeeded by **Jack Vaughn**
- ○ Preceded by **none**: **Director of the Office of Economic Opportunity** 1965 1968: Succeeded by **Bertrand Harding**
- ○ Diplomatic posts
- ○ Preceded by **Charles E. Bohlen**: **U.S. Ambassador to France** 1968 1970: Succeeded by **Arthur K. Watson**
- ○ Party political offices
- ○ Preceded by **Edmund Muskie** *(previous race: 1968)*, **Thomas Eagleton** *(previous candidate: 1972)*[1]: **Democratic Party Vice Presidential candidate** 1972 (lost): Succeeded by **Walter Mondale**
- ○ **Notes and references (URLs online)**
- ○ 1. Eagleton was the original Vice Presidential nominee in 1972 but withdrew from the race and was replaced by Shriver. Muskie was the Vice Presidential nominee in 1968.

A hyperlinked version of this chapter is at http://booksllc.net?q=Sargent%5FShriver

26

SPECIAL OLYMPICS

- Founders: Eunice Kennedy Shriver Anne McGlone Burke
- Founded: 1968
- Headquarters: 1133 19th Street, N.W., Washington, DC, U.S. 20036-3604
- Origins: Camp Shriver
- Staff: Tim Shriver (Chairman and CEO) Stephen M. Carter (Lead Director & Vice Chair) Nadia Comaneci (Vice Chair) Raymond J. Lane (Vice Chair) J. Brady Lum (President and COO) Andrew Robertson (Treasurer)
- Area served: International
- Motto: Let me win. But if I cannot win, let me be brave in the attempt.
- Website: www.specialolympics.org

Special Olympics is an international organization and competition held every two years, alternating between Summer and Winter Games, for people who have intellectual disabilities. There are also local, national and regional competitions in over 150 countries worldwide.

History

The first International Special Olympics Games were held in Chicago in 1968. Anne McGlone Burke, a physical education teacher with the Chicago Park District, began with the idea for a one-time Olympic-style athletic competition for people with special needs. Burke then approached Eunice Kennedy Shriver, head of the Joseph P. Kennedy Jr. Foundation, to fund the event. Shriver encouraged Burke to expand on the idea and the JPK Foundation provided a grant of $25,000. More than 1,000 athletes from across the United States and Canada participated. At the Games, Shriver announced the formation of Special Olympics. Shriver s sister, Rosemary Kennedy, underwent a lobotomy in an effort to alter her personality. The brain damage inflicted by the operation caused a severe permanent intellectual disability. This disability is often credited as Shriver's inspiration to help grow the Special Olympics.

In June 1962, Eunice Kennedy Shriver started a day camp, known as Camp Shriver, for children with intellectual disabilities at her home in Potomac, Maryland. Using Camp Shriver as an example, Shriver promoted the concept of involvement in physical activity and competition opportunities for people with intellectual disabilities. Camp Shriver became an annual event, and the Kennedy Foundation (of which Shriver was Executive Vice President) gave grants to universities, recreation departments and community centers to hold similar camps.

Online image: The crowd at the 2003 Special Olympics World Summer Games Opening Ceremonies in Croke Park, Dublin, Ireland.

In 1971, The U.S. Olympic Committee gave the Special Olympics official approval to use the name "Olympics".

The first International Special Olympics Winter Games were held in February 1977 in Steamboat Springs, Colorado, USA. [1]

In 1988, the Special Olympics was officially recognized by the International Olympic Committee (IOC).

In 1997, Healthy Athletes became an official Special Olympics initiative, offering health information and screenings to Special Olympics athletes worldwide.

On October 30, 2004, President George W. Bush signed into law the "Special Olympics Sport and Empowerment Act," Public Law 108-406. The bill authorized funding for its Healthy Athletes, Education, and Worldwide Expansion programs. [2] Co-sponsored by Representatives Roy Blunt (R-MO), and Steny Hoyer (D-MD), and Senators Rick Santorum (R-PA) and Harry Reid (D-NV), the bills were passed by unanimous consent in both chambers.

In July 2006, the first Special Olympics USA National Games were held at Iowa State University. Teams from all 50 states and the District of Columbia participated. [3]

In 2003 the first Special Olympics World Summer Games to be held outside of the United States took place in Dublin Ireland. Approximately 7000 athletes from 150 countries competed over 18 disciplines. The Dublin games were also the first to have their own opening and closing ceremonies broadcast live, performed by President of Ireland Mary McAleese

In 2008, the Special Olympics and Best Buddies International launched the Spread the Word to End the Word campaign to encourage individuals to stop using the word "retard" in everyday speech.

Participation

More than three million athletes of all ages are involved in Special Olympics sports training and competition in over 170 countries. The organization offers year-round training and competition in 30 Olympic-type summer and winter sports.

The Special Olympics motto is "Let me win. But if I cannot win, let me be brave in the attempt."

See also (online edition)

- Flame of Hope
- Law Enforcement Torch Run
- Olympic Games
- Paralympic Games
- Deaflympics
- Special Olympics Canada
- Special Olympics Great Britain
- Special Olympics USA
- Special Olympics World Games
- Special Hockey

Notes

Websites (URLs online)

- Special Olympics
- Special Olympics Live Internet video coverage of the 2009 Special Olympics games.
- Special Olympics Australia

A hyperlinked version of this chapter is at http://booksllc.net?q=Special%5FOlympics

27

SPECIAL OLYMPICS CANADA

Special Olympics Canada is a national organization created to help people with intellectual disabilities develop self-confidence and social skills through sports training and competition.

About

Special Olympics Canada is dedicated to enriching the lives of Canadians with an intellectual disability through sport. It is a national not-for-profit grassroots organization that provides sport training and competition opportunities through the local sport club to more than 32,000 athletes of all ages and abilities. More than 13,000 trained volunteer coaches are currently involved with Special Olympics, supporting and running programs each day in virtually every community nationwide. This vital human resource also includes more than 12,000 members of the policing community who have supported Special Olympics, largely through the Law Enforcement Torch Run. Special Olympics Canada is part of a global movement and celebrates 40 years in Canada this year (2009). Special Olympics Canada's programs are supported by corporate sponsorship, fundraising activities, government funding as well as individual donors. Special Olympics Canada is structured into regional, provincial and national programs and competitions. National competitions are held every two years, alternating between summer and winter games with Special Olympics World Games held in the year following national games. Canadian athletes have the opportunity to participate along with more than 150 other countries in Special Olympics World Summer or Winter Games through selection in the national team program. Which is very cool.

History

In the early sixties, testing of children with intellectual disabilities revealed that they were only half as physically fit as their non-disabled peers. It was assumed that their low fitness levels were a direct result of mental retardation. A Toronto researcher and professor, Dr. Frank Hayden, questioned this assumption. Working with a control group of children on an intense fitness program, he demonstrated that, given the opportunity, intellectually disabled people could become physically fit and acquire the physical skills necessary to participate in sport. His research proved that low levels of fitness and lack of motor skills development in people with mental handicaps were a result of nothing more than a sedentary life style. In other words, their intellectual disabilities resulted in their exclusion from the kinds of physical activity and sports experience readily available to other children.

Inspired by his discoveries, Dr. Hayden began searching for ways to develop a national sports program for intellectually disabled people. It was a goal he eventually achieved, albeit not in Canada. His work came to the attention of Eunice Kennedy Shriver and the Kennedy Foundation in Washington, D.C., and led to the creation of Special Olympics. The first sports competitions organized under the Special Olympics banner were held at Soldier Field in Chicago in 1968. To ensure that Canada was represented, Dr. Hayden called on an old friend, Harry "Red" Foster.

The late Harry "Red" Foster was an outstanding sportsman, a famous broadcaster, a successful businessman and a humanitarian whose tireless work on behalf of people with an intellectual disability had already brought him international acclaim. Inspired by his mother's devotion to his younger brother, who was both blind and intellectually disabled, Mr. Foster began early in his career to devote much of his time, energy and wealth to addressing the problems faced by individuals with an intellectual disability and their families.

Accompanying a floor hockey team from Toronto to those first Games in Chicago, "Red" was quick to see in Special Olympics a further opportunity to enhance the lives of intellectually disabled Canadians. Upon returning to Canada he set about laying the foundation for the Special Olympics movement. The following summer, 1969, the first Special Olympics Canada event was held in Toronto. From that modest beginning, the Special Olympics movement quickly spread across the country and grew into the national sports organization it is today.

Official Special Olympics Canada Sports

Winter Sports

- o Alpine Skiing
- o Cross Country Skiing
- o Curling
- o Figure Skating
- o Floor Hockey
- o Snowshoeing
- o Speed Skating

Summer Sports

- o Aquatics
- o Athletics (Track & Field)
- o Bowling (5 & 10 Pin)
- o Power-lifting
- o Rhythmic Gymnastics
- o Soccer
- o Softball

Websites (URLs online)

- o Special Olympics Canada

A hyperlinked version of this chapter is at http://booksllc.net?q=Special%
5FOlympics%5FCanada

28

SPECIAL OLYMPICS GREAT BRITAIN

Online image: Logo of the Special Olympics Great Britain

The **Special Olympics Great Britain** take place in Britain every two years, alternating between summer and winter games[1]. They are part of Special Olympics International.

The seventh games took place in 2005 in Glasgow, from 2 July to 9 July. Over 2500 athletes from across Great Britain competed in 23 sports. The Games Village was at the Scotstoun Leisure Centre.

Information on the next summer games in 2009 can be found at Special Olympics Leicester.

References (URLs online)

- o 1. "City to host its second 'games'". BBC News Online. 2007-07-13. Retrieved 2007-07-14.

Websites (URLs online)

○ Official website

A hyperlinked version of this chapter is at http://booksllc.net?q=Special%
5FOlympics%5FGreat%5FBritain

29

SPECIAL OLYMPICS LEICESTER

The **8th Special Olympics GB National Summer Games** will be held in Leicester between the 25 and 31 July 2009. Over 2,700 athletes representing 18 Special Olympics regions across the UK will visit the city of Leicester over the seven day period along with 1,200 coaches and 1,500 volunteers.

The 2,700 athletes will compete in 21 Olympic style competitions across the city & Rutland. Leicestershire County Cricket Club, Leicester City Football Club and Rutland Water are just some of the sporting venues confirmed to host the 2009 Games.

Leicester's landscape has changed dramatically since the city first hosted the Games in 1989. From the rich diversity of its population, to the magnificent ongoing 3 billion regeneration programme, Leicester is a city rising to the challenge on many fronts and between the 25 and 31 July 2009, the eyes of the UK will be firmly placed on the Special Olympics GB athletes as they compete in the National Summer Games.

The city of Leicester is looking to recruit 1,500 volunteers to participate in the Games next year.

A host of celebrities have already offered up their support to the Games next year including Martin Johnson, Gary Lineker, Leicester Tigers, Leicester City FC, and Leicestershire CCC.

Special Olympics National Summer Games is part of Special Olympics GB. Special Olympics is a global organisation that provides year-round sports training and athletic competition to more than 2.25 million children and adults with learning disabilities across the globe. Founded by Eunice Kennedy Shriver, sister of the late President John F Kennedy in 1968, Special Olympics provides people with learning disabilities opportunities to realise their potential, develop physical fitness, demonstrate courage and experience joy and friendship.

Special Olympics Great Britain (SOGB) is the major provider of sporting opportunities for people with a learning disability and provides equality of opportunity for all athletes regardless of ability or degree of disability.

In February 1988, the IOC, the umbrella organization of the Olympic movement, officially recognised Special Olympics as the third Olympic movement alongside the Olympics and Paralympics.

SOGB was established in 1978 as part of Special Olympics Inc. SOGB is a registered charity and a company limited by guarantee and presently offer opportunities to more than 8000 children and adults with a learning disability and will work to expand opportunities to reach a further 10,000 individuals by 2010.

Websites (URLs online)

- ○ Special Olympics Leicester Official Website
- ○ Special Olympics Great Britain
- ○ Voluntary Action Leicester

A hyperlinked version of this chapter is at http://booksllc.net?q=Special%5FOlympics%5FLeicester

30

SPECIAL OLYMPICS NEW JERSEY

Special Olympics New Jersey is a not-for-profit organization that provides sports training and Olympic-type competition in 24 sports for more than 21,000 children and adults with intellectual disabilities at no cost to the participants. It operates year-round.

The organization's mission includes providing continuing opportunities to develop physical fitness, demonstrate courage, experience joy and participate in a sharing of gifts, skills and friendship with their families, other Special Olympics athletes and the community. It was created by the Joseph P. Kennedy, Jr. Foundation and is authorized and accredited by Special Olympics, Inc. for the Benefit of Persons with intellectual disabilities.

Special Olympics believes that through sports training and competition, people with intellectual disabilities are benefited physically, mentally, socially and spiritually; families are strengthened, and the community at large, both through participation and observation, is united in understanding with those with intellectual disabilities in an environment of equality, respect and acceptance.

Athletes' Oath: Let me win. But if I cannot win, let me be brave in the attempt.

Sports

In New Jersey, athletes participate in:

- Alpine Skiing
- Aquatics
- Basketball
- Bocce
- Bowling
- Cross-Country Skiing
- Cycling
- Equestrian
- Figure Skating
- Flag Football
- Floor Hockey
- Golf
- Gymnastics
- Motor Activities Training
- Powerlifting
- Sailing
- Speed Skating
- Snow Boarding
- Snowshoeing
- Soccer
- Softball
- Tennis
- Track & Field
- Volleyball

New Jersey Competition Offerings

Special Olympics New Jersey conducts four major events annually:

- Fall Sports Festival
- Winter Games / Floor Hockey Tournament
- Spring Sports Festival
- Summer Games

Levels of Competition

Athletes advance to higher levels of competition, as described below, through criteria established by the previous level of competition in accordance with Special Olympics policies and procedures.

Area Events

Area events are local events held within the county or counties in the area. Competition must be conducted in compliance with official Special Olympics Rules. Area events may be conducted as qualifiers in order to meet the criteria for advancement to the next level of competition.

Invitational Events

Invitational events may be conducted to include two or more Local Training Programs or Areas. These events do not qualify athletes for advancement in their sport, but simply serve as another competition opportunity.

Sectional Events

Sectional events are conducted as qualifiers in order to meet the criteria for athletes to advance to Chapter level competition. Competition is conducted in compliance with Official Special Olympics Rules. Sectional Events are regional competitions held throughout the state.

Chapter Events

Chapter events are state-wide competitions conducted at the culmination of each sports season and serve as qualifiers to meet the criteria for athletes to advance to the National level of competition. Chapter events are the highest level of competition offered for athletes within the state. Chapter competition is conducted in compliance with Special Olympics rules.

National Games

National Summer Games are conducted every four years. Each Chapter of the United States sends a delegation representing their state. National Games are conducted as qualifiers in order to meet the criteria for athletes to advance to the World Games level of competition.

World Games

World Games are offered every two years on an alternating Winter Games and Summer Games basis. The United States are represented as one delegation under TEAM USA.

In 2009, 24 New Jersey athletes participated in the World Games held in Boise, Idaho. The event drew 3,000 athletes who represented more than 100 countries.[1]

Eligibility

To be eligible to participate in Special Olympics, athletes must be at least 8 years old* and identified by an agency or professional as having one of the following conditions: intellectual disability; a cognitive delay as determined by standardized measures such as intelligence quotient or other generally accepted measures; or a closely related developmental disability, i.e., functional limitations in both general learning and adaptive skills. There is no cost to participate in Special Olympics.

Children ages 2 $\frac{1}{2}$ to 7 are eligible to participate in the Young Athlete Program.

References (URLs online)

- 1. Sparta Independent: From Fredon to the Special Olympics World Games in Idaho February 12, 2009

Websites (URLs online)

- Special Olympics New Jersey Official Web Site
- Law Enforcement Torch Run for Special Olympics New Jersey
- Facebook Fan Page
- Special Olympics, Inc.

A hyperlinked version of this chapter is at http://booksllc.net?q=Special%5FOlympics%5FNew%5FJersey

31

SPECIAL OLYMPICS USA

Online image: Logo of the 2006 Special Olympics USA National Games

The **Special Olympics USA National Games** were first held in 2006, July 2-6, in Ames, Iowa.

2006 Games

The city of Ames and Iowa State University hosted over 3000 athletes from all 50 states to come and compete in 13 competition sports, including gymnastics, basketball, and powerlifting. Over 8000 volunteers were needed to make this event run smoothly. Actor Tom Arnold, originally from Iowa, was the emcee for the Opening Ceremonies, and several other celebrities were at the event as well, including NFL quarterback Kurt Warner and actor Brandon Routh, both also Iowans.

Websites (URLs online)

- o Official Website

Special Olympics.

○ 2006 Special Olympics USA National Games Website

A hyperlinked version of this chapter is at http://booksllc.net?q=Special%
5FOlympics%5FUSA

32

SPECIAL OLYMPICS WORLD GAMES

Online image: The mascot for the Shanghai 2007 Special Olympics, displayed in Pudong in front of the Shanghai Science and Technology Museum.

The **Special Olympics World Games** are an international sporting competition for athletes with intellectual disabilities, organized by Special Olympics.

Like the Olympic Games and the Paralympic Games, the Special Olympics World Games include summer and winter versions, and are held every four years. The first International Special Olympics Summer Games were held in Chicago, Illinois, USA, in 1968. The first International Special Olympics Winter Games were held in February 1977 in Steamboat Springs, Colorado, USA.

In 1991, the name was officially changed from International Special Olympics Summer or Winter Games to Special Olympics World Summer or World Winter Games.

Summer and Winter Games

: *Summer Special Olympics World Games*

○ *Year: Games: Date: Host City: Country*
○ 1968 International Special Olympics Summer Games: I: July 20 1968: Chicago, Illinois: USA
○ 1970 International Special Olympics Summer Games: II: August 13-15 1970: Chicago, Illinois: USA
○ 1972 International Special Olympics Summer Games: III: August 13-18 1972: Los Angeles, CA: USA
○ 1975 International Special Olympics Summer Games: IV: August 8-13 1975: Mt. Pleasant, Michigan: USA
○ 1979 International Special Olympics Summer Games: V: August 8-13 1979: Brockport, New York: USA
○ 1983 International Special Olympics Summer Games: VI: July 12-18 1983: Baton Rouge, Louisiana: USA
○ 1987 International Special Olympics Summer Games: VII: July 31-August 1 1987: South Bend, Indiana: USA
○ 1991 Special Olympics World Summer Games: VIII: July 19-27 1991: Minneapolis & St. Paul, Minnesota: USA
○ 1995 Special Olympics World Summer Games: IX: July 1-9 1995: New Haven, Connecticut: USA
○ 1999 Special Olympics World Summer Games: X: June 26-July 4 1999: Durham, North Carolina: USA
○ 2003 Special Olympics World Summer Games: XI: June 21-29 2003: Dublin: Ireland
○ 2007 Special Olympics World Summer Games: XII: October 2-11 2007: Shanghai: China
○ 2011 Special Olympics World Summer Games: XIII: June 25- July 4, 2011: Athens: Greece

: *Winter Special Olympics World Games*

○ *Year: Games: Date: Host City: Country*
○ 1977 International Special Olympics Winter Games: I: February 5-11 1977: Steamboat Springs, Colorado: USA
○ 1981 International Special Olympics Winter Games: II: March 8-13 1981: Smugglers' Notch and Stowe, Vermont: USA
○ 1985 International Special Olympics Winter Games: III: March 24-29 1985: Park City, Utah: USA
○ 1989 International Special Olympics Winter Games: IV: April 1-8 1989: Reno, Nevada and Lake Tahoe, California: USA
○ 1993 Special Olympics World Winter Games: V: March 20-27 1993: Salzburg and Schladming: Austria
○ 1997 Special Olympics World Winter Games: VI: February 1-8 1997: Toronto and Collingwood, Ontario: Canada
○ 2001 Special Olympics World Winter Games: VII: March 4-11 2001: Anchorage, Alaska: USA
○ 2005 Special Olympics World Winter Games: VIII: February 26 - March 4 2005: Nagano: Japan

o 2009 Special Olympics World Winter Games*: IX: February 6-13 2009: Boise, Idaho: USA

(*) - Sarajevo, Bosnia-Herzegovina, was originally the host city of the 2009 Special Olympics World Winter Games. However, due to "unknown circumstances", the city gave hosting rights back to Special Olympics.

Summer sports

o Aquatics
o Athletics (track and field)
o Badminton
o Basketball
o Bocce
o Bowling
o Cycling
o Equestrian
o Floor Hockey
o Football (Soccer)
o Golf
o Gymnastics
o Judo
o Powerlifting
o Roller Skating
o Sailing
o Softball
o Table Tennis
o Team Handball
o Tennis
o Volleyball

Winter Sports

o Alpine Skiing
o Cross-country skiing
o Figure Skating
o Snowboarding
o Snowshoeing
o Speed Skating
o Floor Hockey

See also (online edition)

o Camp Shriver
o Special Olympics
o Deaflympics
o Paralympic Games
o Olympic Games

- ○ Ancient Olympics
- ○ Flame of Hope

Websites (URLs online)

- ○ Special Olympics

A hyperlinked version of this chapter is at http://booksllc.net?q=Special%
5FOlympics%5FWorld%5FGames

33

STATE FARM HOLIDAY CLASSIC

The **State Farm Holiday Classic**, named after the title sponsor State Farm Insurance, is the largest co-ed high school holiday basketball tournament in the United States with 64 teams (32 boys and 32 girls). Held annually for four days following Christmas, and dubbed "The Best Basketball This Side of March", the Classic is held at numerous college and high school venues throughout Bloomington-Normal, Illinois.

History

The Classic was originated in 1975 and was first called the Illinois State Classic. Normal Community High School was crowned the first boys champion by defeating Chicago Brother Rice, 60-51. Over the next 10 years (through 1985), Lincoln would play in the championship game four times (winning twice) and Galesburg would win four championships, including three straight titles from 1981-83.

In the beginning, the Classic field consisted of a combination of 16 Class A (small school) and Class AA (large school) teams, from all over the state including all four intercity schools. The Classic took a break from 1986 through 1989, but came back in 1990 and was known as the University High Classic. Sherrard was crowned the champ in 1990, and two years later Gridley became the first Class A school to slay the giants and walk away as champion of the Holiday Classic.

Over the years the Classic has seen its share of great individual performances. In 1985, Rockton Hononegah's Jim Shikenjanski averaged nearly 33 points a game, and pulled down 66 rebounds over the course of the tournament. Eight years later in 1993, Mike Robinson of Peoria Richwoods knocked down 18 field goals in one game, while in 1999 Rock Island Alleman's Tyler Ryan killed 9 three pointers for a tournament record. In 1996, Joey Range from Galesburg wowed the crowd with a tournament record 55 points in one game, while Normal U-High's Jeremy Stanton delivered an unselfish 18 assists in one contest. And of course who could forget watching the man-child, Eddy Curry, go from signing autographs in the Shirk Center bleachers to a first round draft pick of the Chicago Bulls right out of South Holland Thornwood.

In 1995, a community volunteer group, spear-headed by tournament president Dan Highland, took over all duties and responsibilities for the tournament. This group, then known as the Classic Organizing Group, Inc. (COG), consisted of leaders from all aspects of the Bloomington-Normal community. The tournament was then called the Bloomington-Normal Holiday Classic, and later took on Converse as its title sponsor in 1996 and 1997.

Major changes implemented at the time included having 32 participating boys teams, and breaking the field into two 16-team sections (Class A and Class AA). All teams would be guaranteed three games, and those teams which went 3-0 would come back on the fourth and final day to determine a champion in each class in the morning. The night session would consist of the two losing teams playing against each other for third place, while the two champs went head to head for the title of Grand Champion. Rockford Boylan won the first Grand Championship game in 1995, defeating Bloomington Central Catholic 74-63. The next year saw Manito Midwest Central, led by Ryan Knuppel, become the second Class A team to win the Classic by defeating Boylan, 64-58, in one of the most exciting games in tournament history.

The Classic also took on a different twist in 1995 by hosting an 8-team girls shootout. This shootout evolved into a 14-team tournament in 1997, and is now a full-fledged 32-team tournament in its 9th season. Galesburg was the first girls Grand Champion in 1997, by overcoming a 17-point deficit and winning a 77-74 thriller over Mendota on a last second three-pointer by Jacque Howard. Galesburg won the first three Grand Championships (1997, 98 & 99) and had a winning streak of 16 games, before being defeated by Urbana in 2000. That same year, Rock Island Alleman became the only Class A team, and the only team other than Galesburg, to win the girls Grand Championship.

In 1999, the Classic got a big shot in the arm with the announcement of State Farm Insurance as its Title Sponsor. The State Farm Holiday Classic, as it is known today, was able to implement a variety of enhancements thanks to this support, and still continues to find new ways to be the best tournament in the nation. By now the event was starting to gain national recognition, and that included adding teams from across the country to its tournament field.

After testing the waters with a team from Milwaukee, WI in 1996, the Classic has seen teams participate from Washington, D.C.; Louisville, KY; Clinton, TN; Lagrange, OH; Mishawaukee, IN; Pittsburgh, PA; New Orleans, LA, Gainesville, FL; Montgomery, AL; Mesa, AZ; St. Charles, MO; Birmingham, AL and Culver, IN.

In 2001, the COG, which is now known as the Classic Tournament, Inc., experimented with eliminating the cross-over Grand Championship game and crowning two girls champions, one in each class. The experiment worked so well that the same idea was implemented into the boys tournament in 2002. By this time, the Grand Championship game had become somewhat anticlimactic for the fans and teams alike, as many times the Class AA teams were to overpowering for the smaller schools. With the new system in place, all teams are now guaranteed four games and championship night has been revived to the point where near capacity Shirk Center crowds are able to witness four consecutive championship games and discover what we know today as "The Best Basketball This Side Of March!"

The Best of the Best... Over the years the Holiday Classic has seen its share of great teams and players. Four of those players have gone onto professional careers in basketball.

- o Melvin McCants of the Los Angeles Lakers (Chicago Mt. Carmel High School)
- o Eddy Curry of the New York Knicks (South Holland Thornwood High School)
- o Brian Cook of the Los Angeles Lakers (Lincoln High School)
- o Latoya Bond of the Charlotte Sting (Urbana High School)
- o Angelina Williams of the Phoenix Mercury (Chicago Washington High School)

The tournament also boasts stars that made their names in other sports.

- o Ogonna Nnamani (Normal U-High) led the Stanford women's volleyball team to the 2004 NCAA National Championship and was a member of the 2004 U.S. Olympic team.
- o Ashlee Pistorius (Normal U-High) was recently named the Honda Sports Award winner as the top collegiate soccer player in the nation, and will play on the USL W-League Boston Renegades this summer.
- o Kayla Pedersen (Mesa Red Mountain, AZ) McDonald's All-American who helped lead the USA 18U national team to the gold medal in 2006.
- o Brittany Johnson (Olney East Richland) became Illinois' all-time leading scorer (boys or girls) during a Holiday Classic game in 2006, and now plays for The Ohio State University.
- o Kevin Roberson (Decatur Eisenhower) played Major League Baseball from 1993-96 with the Chicago Cubs and New York Mets.

o Zach McAllister (Chillicothe IVC) was drafted in 2006 in the third round by the New York Yankees and played this summer for the Gulf Coast League Yankees.

All-Quarter Century Team

In 2003, fans had a chance to vote on the most outstanding performers in the 25 year history of the tournament. The following team was chosen:

- o Brian Cook, Lincoln I 315 votes
- o Eddy Curry, Thornwood I 271 votes
- o Joey Range, Galesburg I 216 votes
- o Gregg Alexander, Lincoln I 143 votes
- o Robbie Minor, Rock Falls I 126 votes
- o Damir Krupaliga, Rockford Boylan I 121 votes

Past Boys Champions

Past Grand Champions

1975 Normal Community 1976 LaSalle-Peru 1977 Lincoln 1978 East Moline 1979 Galesburg 1980 Lincoln 1981 Galesburg 1982 Galesburg 1983 Galesburg 1984 Decatur Eisenhower 1985 Normal Community 1990 Sherrard 1991 Normal UHigh 1992 Gridley 1993 Peoria Richwoods 1994 East Peoria 1995 Rockford Boylan 1996 Manito Midwest Central 1997 Galesburg 1998 Rockford Boylan 1999 South Holland Thornwood 2000 South Holland Thornwood 2001 South Holland Thornwood

Past Class A Champions*

2002 Quincy Notre Dame 2003 Lagrange Keystone, Ohio 2004 Quincy Notre Dame 2005 Hartsburg-Emden 2006 Bloomington Central Catholic 2007 Bloomington Central Catholic 2008 Peoria Christian

Past Class AA Champions*

2002 South Holland Thornwood 2003 Chicago Prosser 2004 Mt. Zion 2005 South Holland Thornwood 2006 South Holland Thornwood 2007 Rockton-Hononegah 2008 Normal Community

Note: Starting in 2002, the Grand Championship game was eliminated and two champions, one in each class, were crowned.

Past Girls Champions

Past Grand Champions

1997 Galesburg 1998 Galesburg 1999 Galesburg 2000 Rock Island Alleman

Past Class A Champions*

2001 Seneca 2002 Normal UHigh 2003 Bloomington Central Catholic 2004 Rock Island Alleman 2005 Chicago John Hope 2006 Olney East Richland 2007 Rochester 2008 Bloomington Central Catholic

Past Class AA Champions*

2001 Geneseo 2002 Peoria Richwoods 2003 Normal Community 2004 Peoria Richwoods 2005 Peoria Richwoods 2006 Bolingbrook 2007 Chicago John Hope 2008 Peoria Richwoods

Note: Starting in 2001, the Grand Championship game was eliminated and two champions, one in each class, were crowned.

State Farm Holiday Classic Scholarship Award

In 2006 the Classic Tournament, Inc., the nonprofit corporation which runs the largest co-ed high school holiday basketball tournament in the nation, selected four winners to be the first-ever recipients of the Holiday Classic Scholarship Award. Each winner received a $1,000 scholarship to go directly to their college of choice to help pay for tuition costs.

Established to recognize and award scholarships to eligible high school seniors who participated in this past year s event, a selection committee chose a male and female winner representing high schools within McLean County, and a male and female winner from high schools outside McLean County.

2009 Holiday Classic Scholarship recipients:

- ○ Kristen Baldwin, Normal Community High School
- ○ Luke Harbers, Normal University High School
- ○ Cora Jeffers, Williamsville High School
- ○ Ross Munsterman, Crescent-Iroquois High School

2008 Holiday Classic Scholarship recipients:

- ○ Brandi Branka, Kankakee Bishop Mac High School
- ○ Andrew Etheridge, Normal Community High School
- ○ Kati Hinshaw, Normal West High School
- ○ Randall Koehler, Roanoke-Benson High School
- ○ Samantha Reich, Park Ridge Maine South High School

2007 Holiday Classic Scholarship recipients:

- Jack Hainline, Stanford Olympia High School
- Patrick Doggett, Crescent Iroquois High School
- Kimberly White, Olney East Richland High School

(Only three awards were given due to a lack of applicants in the McLean County female division)

2006 Holiday Classic Scholarship recipients:

- Matt Pelton, Bloomington Central Catholic High School
- Cherelle Gay, Bloomington High School
- Jordan Christensen, Sherrard High School
- Taylor Baucom, Camp Point Central High School

Ron Knisley Memorial Special Olympics Shootout

On October 13, 2005, the Classic Tournament Inc. lost a very special and vital part of this event when Ron Knisley, Director of Sports and Competition for Special Olympics Illinois lost his battle to cancer. That year, the tournament decided to name the Special Olympics portion of the State Farm Holiday Classic after the man who was responsible for bringing the two groups together.

The shootout, which brings in six area Special Olympics Illinois (SOI) basketball teams as part of championship day at the annual State Farm Holiday Classic basketball tournament, is now known as the Ron Knisley Memorial Special Olympics Shootout. The Shootout traditionally invites six teams who play games on the final day of the tournament on practice courts at the Shirk Center. Then, each of the teams is featured during half-time of the championship games on the final night of the tournament in a 8-minute, running clock exhibition on the main floor.

Past participants in the Shootout include teams from the following programs:

- Beardstown
- Bloomington SOAR
- Champaign-Urbana Special Recreation
- Decatur Park District
- Jacksonville Pathway
- Lincoln Park District
- Pekin IRVSRA
- Peoria Heart of Illinois
- Pontiac Futures
- Princeton Gateway Services

Websites (URLs online)

- State Farm Holiday Classic Official Web site

o *Pantagraph* newspaper – provides extensive tournament coverage

A hyperlinked version of this chapter is at http://booksllc.net?q=State%5FFarm%5FHoliday%5FClassic

TIMOTHY SHRIVER

Timothy Perry Shriver

- o Born: August 29, 1959 (1959-08-29) Boston, Massachusetts[1]
- o Residence: Chevy Chase, Maryland U.S.
- o Education: B.A., M.A., Ph.D.
- o *Alma mater*: St. Albans School The Catholic University of America University of Connecticut
- o Occupation: Chairman and CEO of Special Olympics
- o Political party: Democratic
- o Spouse(s): Linda Potter
- o Children: Sophia Rose Shriver, Timothy Potter Shriver, Samuel Kennedy Potter Shriver, Kathleen Potter Shriver, Caroline Potter Shriver
- o Parents: Sargent Shriver Eunice Kennedy Shriver

Timothy Perry Shriver (born August 29, 1959) is Chairman and CEO of Special Olympics.[2]

Early life and education

Timothy Shriver was born to Sargent Shriver, a former United States Ambassador to France and the Democratic Party's vice-presidential candidate in 1972, and Eunice Kennedy Shriver, the founder of Special Olympics. He was raised as a Catholic[3] along with his siblings, Bobby Shriver, Maria Shriver, Mark Shriver, and Anthony Shriver. He is a member of Kennedy Family through his mother.

Shriver graduated from St. Albans School.[4] He received his bachelor's degree from Yale University in 1981, his master's degree in Religion and Religious Education from The Catholic University of America in 1988,[5] and his Ph.D. in education from the University of Connecticut in 1996.

Career

He served as a high school teacher in the New Haven, Connecticut public school system, and as a counselor and teacher in the University of Connecticut branch of the Upward Bound program for disadvantaged youth. He became a Fellow at the School Development Program at the Yale Child Study Center.

He was instrumental in establishing the Social Development Project at the public schools in New Haven, Connecticut and also established the Collaborative for Academic, Social and Emotional Learning at the University of Illinois at Chicago.

He was the executive producer on *The Ringer*, a co-producer on *Amistad* and the Disney movie *The Loretta Claiborne Story*, and has served as a producer or co-producer on shows for the American Broadcasting Company, the National Broadcasting Corporation, and the TNT cable channel. He is currently a board member of Malaria No More, a New York-based nonprofit that was launched at the 2006 White House Summit with the goal of ending all deaths caused by malaria.

He is currently the Chairman and CEO of Special Olympics.

Call to action for society to stop the degrading use of the "R-word"

As chairman of Special Olympics, Timothy Shriver has campaigned against mocking of and discrimination against participants in Special Olympics. He has specifically argued against use of what he calls "the R word," meaning *retarded*, stating that the word, "retard", is very offensive and people with intellectual disabilities should be respected and treated like all other people.

In 2008, Shriver and supporters called for a boycott of the movie *Tropic Thunder*, claiming that it mocks people with mental disabilities. The movie is written, produced by and stars Ben Stiller. In a commentary for CNN, Shriver wrote in part,

Together with the members of the international coalition, I am asking Steven Spielberg, Stacey Snider, Ben Stiller and the entire "Tropic Thunder" team to stop showing the film, and asking movie theaters and moviegoers to shut this movie out. "Tropic Thunder" is a colossal blunder. Don't show or see "Tropic Thunder."

The degrading use of the word "retard" together with the broader humiliation of people with intellectual disabilities in the film goes way too far. When the R-word is casually bandied about and when bumbling, clueless caricatures designed to mimic the behavior of people with intellectual disabilities are on screen, they have an unmistakable outcome: They mock, directly or indirectly, people with intellectual disabilities. They perpetuate the worst stereotypes. They further exclusion and isolation. They are simply mean.[6]

Personal life

Shriver married Linda Potter (born January 13, 1956)[7] on May 31 1986. They currently reside in Chevy Chase, Maryland with their five children: Sophia Rose Shriver (born June 14, 1987); Timothy Potter Shriver (born December 10, 1988); Samuel Kennedy Potter Shriver (born July 13, 1992); Kathleen Potter Shriver (born March 9, 1994), and Caroline Potter Shriver (born July 18, 1997).

Awards and honors

- Honorary degree from University of Connecticut
- Honorary degree from Niagara University
- Honorary degree from Albertus Magnus College
- The Medal of the City of Athens, Greece
- 1995 Connecticut Citizen of the Year.
- Honorary degree from Loyola University
- Honorary degree from New England College
- The Order de Manuel Amador Guerrera of the Republic of Panama

Board membership

- American Association on Intellectual and Developmental Disabilities
- Board of the Education Commission of the States Compact for Learning and Citizenship
- Council on Foreign Relations
- The Edison Schools Incorporated
- The Frank Porter Graham Child Development Center at the University of North Carolina at Chapel Hill
- Board of Advisors for HealthCorps

See also (online edition)

Siblings of Timothy Shriver:

- Maria Owings Shriver (b. 1955)
- Mark Kennedy Shriver (b. 1964)

- ○ Robert Sargent Shriver III (b. 1954)
- ○ Anthony Paul Kennedy Shriver (b. 1965)

References (URLs online)

- ○ 1. Time Begins Again on Opening Day
- ○ 2. Inspiring Theme Song - Sports - China Travel Community
- ○ 3. Proud to Be a Catholic
- ○ 4. "Linda Potter To Wed Timothy Shriver - New York Times". New York Times. 1985-12-08. Retrieved 2008-06-26.
- ○ 5. The Catholic University of America Office of Alumni Relations
- ○ 6. Shriver, Timothy (2008-08-13). "Commentary: Why 'Tropic Thunder' shouldn't be seen". CNN.com. Retrieved 2009-08-15.
- ○ 7. American Experience | The Kennedys | Kennedy Family Tree | PBS

Websites (URLs online)

- ○ Religion from the Heart: Re-thinking, Re-feeling and Reviving Faith By: Timothy Shriver
- ○ Timothy Shriver at the Internet Movie Database
- ○ Full Biography from the Special Olympics Website
- ○ The Collaborative for Academic, Social, and Emotional Learning
- ○ Malaria No More

A hyperlinked version of this chapter is at http://booksllc.net?q=Timothy%5FShriver

INDEX

A Very Special Acoustic Christmas, 26, 33, 35
A Very Special Christmas, 21, 23, 25, 29, 31, 33, 35, 37
A Very Special Christmas 2, 23, 26, 31
A Very Special Christmas 3, 26, 29, 37
A Very Special Christmas 5, 21, 26, 37
A Very Special Christmas 7, 21, 26
A Very Special Christmas Live, 26, 31, 33
A&M Records, 23, 25, 29, 31, 33, 34, 37, 38
ABC News, 50, 51
activist, 64
Addison's disease, 49
Alan Jackson, 22
Alaska, 90
Albertus Magnus College, 103
Alison Krauss, 22
Alison Moyet, 24
Allmusic, 23, 29, 31–33, 37
Alma mater, 45, 64, 101
Alpine Skiing, 18, 91
Alpine skiing, 12
Alzheimer's disease, 66
Amazon.com, 24, 30, 32, 34, 38
America First, 64
American, 64
American Broadcasting Company, 102

American University, 47
Ames, Iowa, 87
Amistad, 102
An Garda Síochána, 9
Anchorage, 90
Ancient Olympics, 92
Andrew Marshall, 9
Andrew Pulley, 67
Angélique Kidjo, 26
Angels We Have Heard on High, 26
Angie Martinez, 32
Anita Baker, 26
Ann, 30
Anne McGlone Burke, 72
Anthony Paul Kennedy Shriver, 45, 46, 64, 65, 104
Anthony Shriver, 102
Aquatics, 4, 6, 9, 13, 19, 91
Aran Islands, 8
Arbour Hill Prison, 9
archive.org, 50
Aretha Franklin, 30
Arnold Schwarzenegger, 8, 46, 66
Arthur K. Watson, 63, 69
Ashley Tisdale, 36
Asiatic-Pacific Campaign Medal, 64

Special Olympics.

Athens, 19, 53, 90, 103
athletes, 87
Athletics (track and field), 4, 9, 13, 19, 91
Athletics / track and field, 6
Attorney, 64
Austria, 90
Ave Maria, 26, 32
Away in a Manger, 22

B.A., 101
B.B. King, 34
Baby, It's Cold Outside, 26
Bachelor of Science, 46
bachelor's degree, 64, 102
Back Door Santa, 24, 34
Badminton, 4, 6, 9, 14, 19, 91
Baltimore Orioles, 66
Bank of Ireland, 8
Barack Obama, 47
Basketball, 4, 6, 9, 14, 16, 19, 91
basketball, 87, 93
Baton Rouge, Louisiana, 90
BBC News Online, 79
Belfast, 7
Ben Stiller, 102
Benedict XVI, 49
Benjamin Spock, 67
Bertie Ahern, 9
Best Buddies, 48
Best Buddies International, 73
Big Hat, 12
Bill Clinton, 33, 37, 47, 67
Billy Crystal, 5
Birch Bayh, 68
Birmingham Southern College, 16
Bishop, 47
Bloomington-Normal, Illinois, 93
Blue Christmas, 30, 32, 34
Blue Note Records, 26
Bluegrass, 21
Blues Traveler, 32
Bob Berg, 26
Bob Seger, 24
Bobby Shriver, 25, 31, 33, 34, 38, 66, 102
Bocce, 4, 6, 10, 14, 19, 91
Bogus Basin Ski Resort, 18
Boise, 18, 91
Boise, Idaho, 17, 85
Bon Jovi, 24, 25
Bonnie Raitt, 30
Bosnia-Herzegovina, 91
Boston, 49
Boston, Massachusetts, 101
Bowling, 4, 6, 10, 14, 16, 19, 91
boycott, 102

Boyz II Men, 30
Brandon Routh, 87
Brecker Brothers, 26
Brian Cook, 95, 96
Brian Kerr, 9
Brockport, New York, 90
Brookline, 45, 46
Bruce Springsteen, 24, 25
Bryan Adams, 24

Caetano Veloso, 26
California Governor, 46
Calvin Graham, 69
Canada, 48, 53, 90
Canoeing, 20
Canterbury School, 64
Cape Cod Hospital, 49
Carla Bley, 26
Carrie Underwood, 36
Carter Twins, 36
Carter-Finley Stadium, 5
Cary, 6
Cassandra Wilson, 26
Catholic, 65, 102
CD, 22
Centerville, 45, 49
Cesária Évora, 26
Chairman and CEO, 71, 101
Chapel Hill, 5
Charice, 36
Charles Brown, 30
Charles E. Bohlen, 63, 69
Checkers, 20
Chester Beatty Library, 8
Chevy Chase, Maryland, 101, 103
Chicago, 1, 39, 46, 65, 76, 89
Chicago City Council, 40
Chicago, Illinois, 90
Chicago-Kent College of Law, 39
Chick Corea, 26
Children, Go Where I Send Thee, 32
China, 13, 57
Chris Cornell, 32
Christmas, 35
Christmas (Baby Please Come Home), 24, 36, 38
Christmas All Over Again, 30
Christmas Don't Be Late (Chipmunk Song), 34
Christmas in Hollis, 24, 38
Christmas Is the Time to Say I Love You, 34
Christmas music, 21, 23, 25, 29, 31, 33, 37
Christmas songs, 35
City High, 34
Civitan International, 48
Claim Jumper, 58

Clinton, Bill, 69
CNN, 102
CNN.com, 104
Colbie Caillat, 36
Collingwood, 90
Colorado, 89
commemorative, 47
commemorative coin issued by the Central Bank
    of Ireland, 9
Compilation album, 21, 23, 29, 31, 33, 35
compilation albums, 21, 25
Connecticut, 3, 103
Convent of the Sacred Heart, 46
Cook County, Illinois, 39
Council on Foreign Relations, 103
Country, 21
country, 35
Cricket, 14
Croke Park, 7, 8, 72
Cross-country Skiing, 18
Cross-country skiing, 12, 91
Cycling, 4, 6, 10, 14, 19, 91
cycling, 3
Cyndi Lauper, 30

Dallek, Robert, 50
Dame of Malta, 40
Dan Tyminski, 22
Darlene Love, 30, 34
Dave Koz, 26
Dave Matthews, 32
David Lenz, 48
Deaflympics, 73, 91
Debbie Gibson, 30
Deep Forest, 26
Delta Kappa Epsilon, 64
Democrat, 47
Democratic, 45, 46, 63, 64, 101
Democratic Party, 64
Democratic Party Vice Presidential candidate,
    69
Democratic Party's, 102
Democrats for Life of America, 47
Denis O'Brien, 9
DePaul University, 39
Devens, Massachusetts, 65
diabetes, 53
Diana Krall, 26
Dianne Reeves, 26
Dido, 34
Director of the Office of Economic Opportunity,
    63
Director of the Peace Corps, 63
Discogs, 32
discrimination, 102

Disney, 102
District of Columbia, 65, 72
Do You Hear What I Hear, 36
Do You Hear What I Hear?, 24
documentary film, 67
Dollar Mountain, 18
Donna de Varona, 51
Dorothy Hamill, 49
Down syndrome, 49
Dr. John, 26
Dragon Boat, 14
DSG, 46
Dublin, 7, 72, 73, 90
Dublin Castle, 8
Durham, 5
Durham, North Carolina, 90

Earl Scruggs, 22
Eddy Curry, 94–96
Edmund Muskie, 69
Edward Kennedy, 67
Edward M. Burke, 40
Edward M. Kennedy, 47
Eleven, 32
Eli Jacobs, 66
Eliane Elias, 26
Ellen McCormack, 68
emcee, 87
England, 46
entrepreneur, 9
Enya, 32
Equestrian, 4, 6, 10, 14, 19, 91
Eric Clapton, 38
Estonia, 41, 43
Estonia at the Olympics, 44
Estonia at the Paralympics, 44
Ethel Kennedy, 64
Eunice Kennedy, 39, 65
Eunice Kennedy Shriver, 64, 71, 72, 101, 102
Eurythmics, 24
Eve 6, 34
Everette Harp, 26
Experiment in International Living, 64
Extreme, 30

faithless elector, 67
Federal Industrial Institution for Women, 46
Feminists for Life of America, 47
Figure Skating, 18, 91
Figure skating, 12
figure skating, 17
Find a Grave, 51
First Lady, 33, 37, 48
Flag Football, 84
Flag of Estonia, 41

Flag of Mexico, 61
Flame of Hope, 9, 58, 59, 73, 92
Floor Hockey, 14, 18, 20, 84, 91
Floor hockey, 12, 62
football, 8
Football (Soccer), 4, 14, 20, 91
Football (soccer), 10
Football / soccer, 6
foster parents, 40
Fourplay, 26
Frank Church, 67
Frank Sinatra, 30
Fred R. Harris, 68
Frederick Banting, 53
Fried, Frank, Harris, Shriver & Jacobson, 66
Frosty the Snowman, 22
Fultondale High School, 16
Fultondale Wildcats, 16
funeral mass, 67

Gabriel's Message, 24
Gaelic football, 9
Garner, 6
Gary Lineker, 82
Genre, 21, 23, 29, 31, 33, 35, 37
George Duke, 26
George McGovern, 46, 66, 67
George W. Bush, 69, 72
George Wallace, 67
Gilberto Gil, 26
Gipsy Kings, 27
Give Me One Reason, 38
Glasgow, 79
Gloriana, 36
Go Tell It on the Mountain, 26
God Rest Ye Merry Gentlemen, 27
Golf, 4, 6, 9, 10, 14, 20, 91
Governor, 47
grades K-12, 48
Great Britain, 79
Greece, 19, 53, 103
Gymnastics, 4, 6, 10, 14, 20, 91
gymnastics, 87

Hakuba, 12
Halloween, 16
Halo Display, 48
Handball, 6
Hark
    The Herald Angels Sing, 36
Harry Reid, 72
Have Yourself A Merry Little Christmas, 36
Have Yourself a Merry Little Christmas, 24, 26
Head Start, 65
Henry M. Jackson, 67

Herb Alpert, 25, 26
Herbie Hancock, 26
high school, 93
Hillary Rodham Clinton, 33, 37
Holly Cole, 26
Hootie & the Blowfish, 32
Hot Hot Hot, 34
Hu Jintao, 13
Hubert Humphrey, 68
hurdles, 3
Hyannis, 45, 49

I Saw Mommy Kissing Santa Claus, 24
I Saw Three Ships, 32
I'll Be Home For Christmas, 22
I'll Be Home for Christmas, 26
ice-skating, 49
Idaho, 17, 91
Idaho Center, 17
Illinois, 1, 65, 89
Illinois Governor, 39
Illinois Supreme Court, 39, 40
insulin, 53
intellectual disabilities, 71, 75, 76, 83, 89
intelligence quotient, 86
intercollegiate athletics, 48
International Olympic Committee, 72
Internet Movie Database, 51, 104
Interscope Records, 33, 37
investor, 66
Iowa, 87
Iowa State University, 72, 87
Iraq, 8
Ireland, 7
Irish Defence Forces, 8
ISBN, 24, 50, 68, 69
It Came Upon the Midnight Clear, 26

Jaak Jõerüüt, 44
Jack Vaughn, 63, 69
Jacqueline Kennedy Onassis, 64
James Thompson, 39
Japan, 8, 11, 90
Jean Kennedy Smith, 47
Jeff Lorber, 26
Jefferson County, Alabama, 15
Jerry Brown, 67
Jerry Moss, 25
Jim Beard, 26
Jim Edgar, 40
Jimmy Carter, 67
Jimmy Iovine, 23, 25, 29
Jingle Bell Rock, 30, 36
Jingle Bells, 22, 26
Joan Kennedy, 64

Job Corps, 65
Joe Biden, 17
Joel Gallen, 33, 34
John Cougar Mellencamp, 24
John F. Kennedy, 46, 63, 65
John F. Kennedy Presidential Library & Museum, 50
John G. Schmitz, 67
John Hospers, 67
John McLaughlin, 26
John Popper, 34, 38
John Scofield, 26
Jon Bon Jovi, 8, 30, 33, 34, 38
Jonny Lang, 32
Joseph Kennedy, Sr., 65
Joseph P. Kennedy, Jr. Foundation, 46
Joseph P. Kennedy, Sr., 45, 46
Joshua Redman, 27
Judo, 10, 14, 20, 91
Julius Hobson, 67
Junichiro Koizumi, 11
juvenile delinquency, 46

Kayaking, 10, 14
Keith Haring, 24, 25
Keith Murray, 32
Kellie Pickler, 35, 36
Kennedy Family, 102
Kennedy family, 45, 46, 50, 64
Kings Hall, 7
Kosovo, 8
Kristinia Debarge, 36
Kurt Warner, 87

Label, 21, 23, 29, 31, 33, 37
Lake Tahoe, 90
Lalah Hathaway, 27
Larry Lucchino, 66
Last Christmas, 36
Latin American, 57
Law Enforcement Torch Run, 53, 73
Leicester City FC, 82
Leicester Tigers, 82
Leicestershire CCC, 82
Leighton Meester, 36
Let It Snow, 26, 36
Let It Snow, Let It Snow, Let It Snow, 22
Lieutenant, 64
Linda Jenness, 67
List of Presidential Medal of Freedom recipients, 47
List of United States political appointments that crossed party lines, 68
Little Drummer Boy, 34, 36
Little Red Rooster, 34

Liu Xiang, 13
Live album, 37
LL.B., 64
Lleyton Hewitt, 9
Lloyd Bentsen, 68
London, 46, 50
London, Ontario, 53
Loretta Claiborne, 3, 48
Los Angeles Times, 51
Los Angeles, CA, 90
Lost Highway, 22
Lost Highway Records, 21
Lou Rawls, 26
Loyola University, 103
Luther Vandross, 30
Lyndon B. Johnson, 63

M-Wave, 11, 12
M.A., 101
México, 61
Macy Gray, 34
Madonna, 24, 25
Malaria No More, 102
Manchester United, 8
Manhattanville College, 46
marathon, 3
Marcus Miller, 27
Maria, 66
Maria High School, 39
Maria Owings Shriver, 45, 46, 64, 65, 103
Maria Shriver, 46, 102
Mark Kennedy Shriver, 45, 46, 64, 65, 103
Mark Ledford, 26
Mark Shriver, 102
Martin Johnson, 82
Marty Stuart, 22
Mary Ann G. McMorrow, 40
Mary Davis, 9
Mary J. Blige, 32, 38
Mary McAleese, 7, 9, 73
Maryland, 6
Maryland Constitution and Bill of Rights at Maryland's Constitutional Convention of 1776, 64
Mase, 32
Mass, 65
Massachusetts, 45, 46
Massachusetts General Hospital, 49
master's degree, 102
MATP, 10
McCall, ID, 18
Medium Wave, 9
mental retardation, 48
Merchandise Mart, 65
Merry Christmas Baby, 24, 30, 34, 38

Mexico, 61
Mexico at the Olympics, 62
Michael Bolton, 30
Michael Franks, 26
Mick O'Dwyer, 9
Miley Cyrus, 36
Milton Shapp, 68
Minneapolis, 90
Mino Cinelu, 26
Mitchel Musso, 36
Mo Udall, 67
mocking, 102
Morning Edition, 51
Morton Stadium, 7
Mountjoy Prison, 9
Mt. Pleasant, Michigan, 90
Muhammad Ali, 8
Mure, 12

Nadia Comaneci, 71
Nagano, 11, 90
Nagano, Nagano, 11
Nancy Wilson, 30
Natalie Merchant, 32
National Archives and Records Administration,
    50
National Basketball Arena, 7
National Broadcasting Corporation, 102
National Collegiate Athletic Association, 48, 50
National Institute of Child Health and Human
    Development, 47, 50
National Institutes of Health, 47
National Portrait Gallery, 48
National Public Radio, 51
Nelson Mandela, 8
New England College, 103
New Haven, 3
New Haven, Connecticut, 90, 102
New Milford, Connecticut, 64
New York, 46, 47
New York City, 46, 65
New York Times, 104
Newbridge, County Kildare, 8
newspaper, 9
NFL, 87
No Doubt, 25, 32
Noel
    Noel, 34
Norah Jones, 22
North Carolina, 5
North Carolina Central University, 5
North Carolina State University, 5
Northern District of Illinois, 39
not-for-profit organization, 83
Notable Names Database, 50

Nozawaonsen, 12

O Christmas Tree, 30
O Come All Ye Faithful, 22, 34
O come, O come, Emmanuel, 26
O Holy Night, 22, 26, 30, 32, 38
O Tannenbaum, 26
of counsel, 66
Office of Economic Opportunity, 69
Ogonna Nnamani, 95
Oklahoma, 58
Olympic Flame, 53, 54
Olympic Games, 53, 54, 59, 73, 89, 91
Olympic Torch Relay, 57
Olympics, 11
Olympics Games, 49
Omnibus Press, 24
ongoing war, 8
Ontario, 90
Onyx, 32
Order of St. Gregory the Great, 48

Panama, 103
Papa Wemba, 26
papal knighthood, 48
Paralympic Games, 73, 89, 91
Paralympics, 11, 54
Park City, 90
Pat Green, 22
Patricia Kennedy Lawford, 47
Patrick Kielty, 8
Patti Smith, 32
Patty Loveless, 22
Paul Young, 30
PBS, 67
PDF, 50
Peace Corps, 46, 64, 65, 69
Penguin Books, 50
Pennsylvania, 47
Ph.D., 101, 102
physical fitness, 83
Pitch & putt, 10
Pittsboro, 6
platform, 47
Please Come Home for Christmas, 22, 30, 38
podcast, 51
Police Service of Northern Ireland, 9
politician, 64
Pope Benedict XVI, 48
Pope Pius XII, 48
Potomac, Maryland, 72
Powder, 34
Powerlifting, 4, 6, 10, 14, 20, 91
powerlifting, 3, 87
President, 33, 37

President of Ireland, 9, 73
Presidential Medal of Freedom, 48, 67
Pretenders, 24
Prime Minister, 11
pro-choice, 47
pro-life movement, 47
Producer, 23, 29, 31, 33
Puff Daddy, 32
Purchase, 46
Purple Heart, 64

quarterback, 87
Qwest Arena, 18

Radio Telefís Éireann, 9
Raleigh, 5
Ralph Stanley, 22
Randy Travis, 30
Reba McEntire, 22
reggae fusion, 35
Reno, Nevada, 90
Republic of Ireland, 8
Republican, 47, 66
Requiem Mass, 49
retarded, 102
Rev Run, 32
Rhonda Vincent, 22
Richard Nixon, 63, 66, 67
Rick Santorum, 72
Rick Schroder, 69
Ricky Skaggs, 22
Riverdance, 8
Robert Byrd, 67
Robert F. Kennedy, 46
Robert P. Casey, 47
Robert Sargent Shriver, 29
Robert Sargent Shriver III, 45, 46, 64, 65, 104
Robert Sargent Shriver, Jr., 45, 46
Rockin' Around The Christmas Tree, 36
Rockin' Around the Christmas Tree, 30, 38
Roehampton, 46
Roger Rasheed, 9
Roller Skating, 4, 14, 20, 91
Roller skating, 6, 10
roller skating, 7
Roman Catholic, 45, 46, 64
Roman Catholic church, 40
Ronald Reagan, 48
Ronnie Spector, 30
rosary, 65
Rose Fitzgerald, 46
Rose Kennedy, 45
Rosemary Kennedy, 47, 72
Roy Blunt, 72
Roy Keane, 8

Royal Dublin Society, 7
RTÉ Radio 1, 9
Run D.M.C., 24, 25, 30, 38
Run Rudolph Run, 24, 34

Sailing, 6, 10, 14, 20, 91
Saint Patrick's Cathedral, 46
Salt N' Pepa, 32
Salzburg, 90
Sam Bush, 22
Sandy Lyle, 9
Santa Baby, 24, 32, 36
Santa Claus Is Coming to Town, 24, 26, 30, 38
Sarajevo, 91
Sargent Shriver, 101, 102
Schladming, 90
Scotstoun, 79
Scroll and Key, 64
Sean Kingston, 35, 36
series, 21, 23, 29, 31, 33
Severiano Ballesteros, 9
sexual abuse, 40
Shanghai, 13, 90
Shanghai Stadium, 13
Shanghai, China, 58
Sheryl Crow, 32, 34, 38
Shriver, 91
Shriver, Maria, 68
Silent Night, 22, 24, 30, 32, 34, 36
silver dollar, 47
Silver Spring, Maryland, 67
Sinéad O'Connor, 30
Sleigh Ride, 30
Smithsonian Institution, 48
SMOM, 39
Smugglers' Notch, 90
Snoop Doggy Dogg, 32
Snow Boarding, 84
Snowboarding, 12, 18, 91
Snowshoe, 12
Snowshoeing, 18, 91
Soccer, 9
social worker, 46
sociology, 46
Softball, 4, 6, 14, 20, 91
Soldier Field, 1, 76
son-in-law, 47
South Bend, Indiana, 90
South Side, 39
Special Hockey, 73
Special Olympics, 21, 23, 25, 29, 31, 33, 35, 37, 39, 46, 50, 51, 53–55, 57, 58, 65, 66, 75, 79, 82, 83, 89, 91, 98, 101, 102
Special Olympics Canada, 73

Special Olympics Great Britain, 73, 82
Special Olympics Leicester, 79
Special Olympics USA, 73
Special Olympics World Games, 11, 41, 53, 58, 59, 61, 73, 86
Special Olympics World Summer Games, 3
Speed Skating, 91
Speed skating, 12, 18
Spiro Agnew, 66, 67
sporting, 89
sports, 75
Sports Illustrated, 48
Sportsman of the Year, 48
Spread the Word to End the Word, 73
squat, 3
SR-71, 34
St. Albans School, 101, 102
St. Patrick's Cathedral, 65
St. Paul, Minnesota, 90
Stanford University, 45, 46
Stanley Clarke, 26
State Farm Insurance, 93
Steamboat Springs, 89
stem-cell research, 66
Steny Hoyer, 72
Steps Ahead, 26
Steve Swallow, 26
Steve Winwood, 32
Steven Spielberg, 102
Stevie Nicks, 24, 25, 34
Stevie Wonder, 5, 34
Sting, 24, 32
Stossel, Scott, 69
Stowe, 90
Sun Valley, 18
Susan B. Anthony List, 47

Table Tennis, 4, 14, 20, 91
Table tennis, 6, 10
Taoiseach, 9
Team Handball, 14, 20, 91
Team handball, 10
Ted, 49
Ted Kennedy, 68
Tennis, 4, 6, 9, 10, 14, 20, 91
Terry Sanford, 68
Tevin Campbell, 30
The Associated Press, 50, 51
The Boston Globe, 51
The Catholic University of America, 101, 102
The Christmas Song, 26, 30, 32, 36
The Corrs, 8
The Coventry Carol, 24
The Daily Telegraph, 51
The Little Drummer Boy, 24, 26

The Nation, 50
The New York Times, 47, 50, 68
The Pointer Sisters, 24
The Ringer, 102
The Smashing Pumpkins, 32
The Washington Post, 50
The Wild Magnolias, 26
Theodora Nathan, 67
Theodore Roosevelt Award, 48
Theodore Roosevelt Award (NCAA), 51
This Christmas, 34
Thomas Eagleton, 64, 66, 69
Thomas J. Anderson, 67
Tift Merritt, 22
Tim Reynolds, 32
Tim Shriver, 71
Time Magazine, 68
Time magazine, 66
Timothy Perry Shriver, 45, 46, 64, 65
TNT, 102
Tom Arnold, 87
Tom Petty & the Heartbreakers, 34
Tom Petty and the Heartbreakers, 30
Toomas Hendrik Ilves, 44
Toronto, 76, 90
Tracy Chapman, 32, 38
Tropic Thunder, 102
Twelve Days of Christmas, 26

U.S., 71, 101
U.S. Ambassador to France, 46, 69
U.S. ambassador to France, 66
U.S. Ambassador to Ireland, 47
U.S. coin, 47
U.S. Conference of Catholic Bishops, 40
U.S. Congress, 48
U.S. Court of Appeals for the 7th Circuit, 39
U.S. Justice Department, 46
U.S. Mint, 51
U.S. Olympic Committee, 72
U.S. President, 46
U.S. Senator, 46
U.S. State Department, 46
U.S. Supreme Court, 65
U.S. vice president, 64
U2, 8, 24, 25
United States, 5, 8, 17, 45, 93
United States Ambassador to France, 46, 63, 102
United States Navy, 64
United States of America, 64
United States presidential election, 1972, 67
University of Connecticut, 101–103
University of Illinois at Chicago, 102
University of North Carolina at Chapel Hill, 5, 103

University of Utah, Salt Lake City, 48
Upward Bound, 65, 102
USA, 3, 89
Utah, 90

Vanessa Hudgens, 36
Vanessa Williams, 30, 38
varsity letter, 48
Vermont, 90
Vice Presidential, 66
vice-presidential, 46
Vicki, 25
Vicki Iovine, 29
Vicki Kennedy, 64
VISTA, 65
Vocal Sampling, 26
Volleyball, 4, 6, 10, 14, 16, 20, 91

W., 69
Walter Mondale, 69
War on Poverty, 65
Washington, D.C., 33, 37, 47, 66
Washington, DC, 71
washingtonpost.com, 50
We Three Kings, 26, 32
We Wish You a Merry Christmas, 26
West Haven, 3
Westminster, Maryland, 63, 64
What Child Is This, 26, 30, 38
What Christmas Means to Me, 30
White Christmas, 30, 34
White House, 51, 102
White Ring, 12
Whitney Houston, 24, 25
Wichita, Kansas, 57
William Cohen, 51
Willie Nelson, 22, 25
Wilson Phillips, 30
Winter Wonderland, 22, 24, 26, 36
WJAR, 50, 51
women's shelter, 46
World War II, 64
World War II Victory Medal, 64
Wyclef Jean, 34
Wynonna, 22

Yale Bowl, 3
Yale Daily News, 64
Yale Law School, 64
Yale University, 64, 102
Yamanouchi, 12
Yomo Toro, 26

Zakir Hussain, 26
Zurab Tsereteli, 45

LaVergne, TN USA
28 June 2010
187669LV00005BA/167/P

Singing on the *Britain's Got Talent* tour, I wore the same dress as I did for the final.

Above: Getting used to receiving visitors at my door, with Frankie, who came up from London to help me.

Below: My mother painted this portrait of me in my pram from a photo.

Above: The clock I bought for my mother with my prize money from the only singing competition I have ever won!

Above and right: The nerve-racking semi-final of *Britain's Got Talent*.

Left: Piers Morgan was the perfect presenter for my television special.

Right: I've been lucky enough to travel all over Europe. Here I am singing at the Sanremo Festival in Italy.

Below: A cold November morning in Rockefeller Plaza, New York, when I launched my debut album.

Who I was born to be!

Below: Singing with Elaine Paige on my television special.

Arriving at Los Angeles airport before my first solo performance.

Right: The badge my dedicated fans made for my Tokyo concert.

東京 日本 TOKYO JAPAN

日本武道館

翼をください Wings to Fly

Susan Boyle

Nippon Budokan
April 1st, 2010
2010年4月1日

Above: The legendary Budokan in Tokyo.

Right: The unique and amazing handmade quilt my fans presented to me in New York.

Left: Shibuya crossing in Tokyo. Even in sunglasses I was recognized wherever I went!

Below: Reading my birthday cards, 1 April 2010.

Below: The beautiful birthday cake with a sugar replica of my album that I shared with my fans in Tokyo.

Above: A very proud moment with conductor Masahiko Enkoji and members of the Yomiuri Nippon Symphony Orchestra after performing at the Budokan.

Below: Another great honour was meeting Cardinal Keith O'Brien.

admit that I had made the semi-finals. If I'd thought that the furore would die down, I was wrong again.

I have always struggled under pressure. My brain doesn't seem to have the same filtering system as other people's when it has too much information to deal with, so I find it very difficult to sort out for myself what I should be concerned about and what doesn't really matter. It's as if everything has the same weight, and it's all stacking up inside my head until there's no room any more.

In a world that was suddenly strange to me, the only thing that was familiar was my religion. I've always believed that if you put your life in God's hands, he will look after you. In my prayers to Our Lady, the simple truth of my devotion was revealed, the assertion of my faith like pure, cool, holy water rinsing through my mind.

My former teacher, Frank Quinn, who had volunteered his support at the beginning, was becoming a great friend. He is a devout Catholic himself and in my conversations with him about spirituality, I felt reunited with what really matters. He encouraged me to believe in myself, as he always had done in class.

Apart from church, the only place I could find peace of mind was when I was singing. From the earliest moments at primary school, singing has always been a calm space for me. On the way into my coaching once a week in London, I was chased by a whirlwind of paparazzi, and I was chased on the way out again. The hours spent inside with Yvie were the eye of the hurricane.

A few months later Andy Stephens, the man who was to become my manager, said something to me that made a great deal of sense, and I wish he'd been looking after me at the time.

'You can be as determined as you like not to change who you are, Susan, but you have no control whatsoever on how people behave towards you.'

That was one of the things I was finding very confusing. People who'd never taken much notice of me before were suddenly my best friends. My family didn't change their way of thinking about me – I was still the baby sister – but that was causing problems too. My brothers John and Gerard decided to express their opinion that I was getting too big for the show. I know that they were trying to look after me and to make sure that I benefited from my moment in the spotlight. None of us knew how long it was going to last. But they shouldn't have made those comments in the press because nobody likes a big-head, and it gave the press just the sniff of controversy they needed once they'd exhausted every angle of the makeover debate. There was no way I was ever going to drop out of the show. I knew it was the chance of my life. I didn't want to annoy Simon Cowell. But the last thing I wanted to do was to cause any conflict within my family.

My acting training came in useful as I tried to disguise my inner turmoil, but some friends and members of my family could see what was happening and were worried about me. They knew from previous experience that when I go quiet it's often an indication that there's a storm brewing. It was suggested that I take someone with me when it came to the semi-finals, but nobody could agree who would be best and, since none of them had any experience of London themselves, it would have been the blind leading the blind. I thanked everybody for their concern and made the decision to go on my own.

When I finally arrived in my room at the Wembley Plaza Hotel and closed the door behind me, I had the definite sense that I was at the beginning of a new phase of my life. Here I was, in London, on my own, doing something that I'd achieved all by myself. It's probably how students feel when they first arrive at university. As I hung my clothes up in the cupboard, bounced up and down on the bed to test how comfortable it was, then checked out the freebies of shampoo and conditioner in the bathroom, the great rush of independence felt fantastic. I had finally left home, and here I was, in the big smoke. Yes, it was scary, but every time I got a frisson of fear I tried to remember what Frank Quinn was always telling me:

'Susan, believe in yourself. You are the person writing your story.'

* * *

My niece Kirsty came up to the hotel for a drink that first evening. The bar was quiet and we were able to have a good chat together. I was aware out of the corner of my eye of a couple of people recognizing me. One man eventually plucked up the courage to come over. He told me that he and his wife were rooting for me, and that was great to hear. I thanked him for that. Otherwise we were left undisturbed; in fact, that first night, the hotel was a lot quieter than my home in Blackburn had been in recent weeks. The anonymity made a pleasant change. I slept fairly well and woke up to a fine morning. It was the first day of my new life of independence and summer had come early. I went downstairs for my breakfast and ate in peace. A car picked me up to take me to the studios near by.

As somebody who likes walking, I didn't much appreciate constantly travelling around in cars. Walking is a good way of getting to know a place. Even though I'd been down to London many times now, the city didn't feel any more familiar to me than it had on that first trip on our way to Lourdes. When we drove into the centre of town from the airport, I could see beautiful parks and, since the reveal day in February, the wintry black skeletons of trees had exploded with vibrant green foliage and pillowy pink blossom. I would have liked to explore those gravel avenues fringed with brilliant flowerbeds and to throw bread to the ducks on the lakes.

There's not a lot of green space in Wembley. The hotel was very near Wembley Stadium, and the area around is geared to match days and gigs at Wembley Arena. When there's nothing on, it's a deserted urban landscape. In the air-conditioned car, I craned my neck to look up at the silver arch towering over the huge grey stadium and gazed at the acres of empty concrete that sparkled in the blistering sunshine.

The song 'Memory' was the obvious choice for me to sing in the semi-final because it is so closely associated with Elaine Paige and she was the singer I had declared I wanted to emulate. It is not just her voice that I admire, but the force of character she brings to a song. There was also the small matter of the song coming from *Cats*, and the world had gone mad for Pebbles, so that added an extra dimension.

Singing the song for the first time in the television studio, I noticed some people arriving at the back and thought to myself, 'Calm down, Susan!'

All the excitement must be making me hallucinate, because the man looked exactly like Andrew Lloyd Webber. But I wasn't seeing things. Lord Andrew Lloyd Webber had come to hear me sing his song. I was shaking when I was introduced to him. He's been part of my life since the early seventies when I first heard *Jesus Christ Superstar*. Whatever else happened, I thought excitedly, I had met one of my heroes and nobody could take that away from me.

Back at the hotel, the other contestants in my semi-final, who hadn't had so far to travel, had begun to arrive and the paparazzi had got wind of us all turning up, so the lobby was a much busier place.

We were a mixed bunch: Nick Hell, a horror-movie of a man on the stage, but a surprisingly ordinary guy in person; a lissom belly dancer called Julia Naidenko; the two dancing lads called Faces of Disco, who'd been in my group on the reveal day; Darth Jackson, who was a cross between Darth Vader and Michael Jackson (only on *Britain's Got Talent*!); Sue Son, the classical violinist who had been persuaded to drop her friend and perform solo; the wee lassie, Natalie Okri, who had also been in my group when we were told we were through to the semi-final; and, of course, Diversity. Because we were going to be the first to go to the public vote, the spirit among us all was not competitive so much as we're-all-in-this-together. A live show is very different from something that's pre-recorded, because you have only one chance – you can't do it again, so it is essential to make sure it is right.

When you first see your own dressing room, it's amazing because you really do have your name on the door and there really are lights round the mirror, like in *A Star is Born*. As soon as the runner closed the door and left me there on my own, I couldn't stop myself doing my little running-on-the-spot dance of joy, which always happens when I'm thrilled to bits. When the designer arrived with the gown that had been specially made for me, I felt like a wee lassie with a dressing-up box. I was a larger lady then than I am now, and there was a wee tiny bra inside the dress. I didn't know how I was going to fit into it, but it was made to measure, so it went on snugly. When I looked at myself in the mirror, I hardly recognized the sophisticated lady grinning back at me in bronze brocade, with bronze shoes to match.

Getting dressed wasn't just about putting on beautiful clothes, it was like putting on a new persona. As I waited for the screens to part on the first dress rehearsal, I no longer felt like Susan Boyle, the wee wifey with a wiggle, I felt like Susan Boyle, the performer. Unfortunately, the elegant effect was somewhat marred when I put my best bronze-slippered foot forward and slid all the way down the runway. I just about managed to stay on my feet, but let's say it wasn't the most graceful entrance, but it was only the rehearsal, so we all had a good laugh about that.

I was last in the running order, so I spent a lot of time during the rehearsal days waiting in my dressing room for my call. Dressing rooms are usually sound-proofed so you can practise singing without disturbing anyone, and there's normally no window, for the obvious reason that you don't want people, or cameras, looking in. After a while it can start to feel a wee bit airless and claustrophobic. Sometimes I went for a walk up and down the backstage corridors to see if there was anyone to have a chat to, but the production team all have their earphones on so that they can hear the director's instructions. The other competitors were friendly enough when our paths crossed, but people had their own preparations to make, their own nerves to keep under control, and they generally had their families with them.

There wasn't the opportunity to get out of the studio for a walk and a breath of fresh air because you never knew when you were going to be needed. Besides, I was wary in case there were photographers outside. It's not that I object to having my photograph taken. I recognize it's part of the job. But going for a stroll to clear your head is not the same as walking up the street with a swarm of photographers buzzing round you.

In the evenings, when we'd finished at the studios and were taken back to the hotel, there were bigger crowds of fans and paparazzi to negotiate each night. The acts from the other semi-finals had begun to arrive to rehearse too and the lobby began to resemble a scrum. I was interrupted so much in the restaurant that I was barely able to eat my food, and there wasn't any privacy in my room either, because by this time the photographers had found out where I was and were staying in the hotel opposite with their telephoto lenses trained on my bedroom, hoping to get a shot of me in my nightie! I had to have the curtains drawn all the time.

The days were very long because I was going from one windowless room to another. My throat was beginning to feel a wee bit dry and scratchy, as if I had a cold coming on.

Be careful what you wish for, Susan!

All the times in my life when I wished that people would take some notice of me, and now there were dozens of people photographing me and clamouring for my autograph, but I'd never felt more lonely in my life. I'd usually been happy enough in my own company, or when it was just me and Pebbles, but, away from the comforts of home, I had to admit that I wasn't really coping very well by myself.

I told myself that I'd elected not to have anyone from my family with me. Some of them were going to come down to be in the audience on Sunday. I wanted them to see me perform and be proud. In the meantime, for once in my life I was going to do something by myself and show everybody that I was capable. I was a grown woman of forty-eight. I'd achieved this opportunity without anyone else's help and I was going to go as far as I could without anyone's help. I didn't want everyone else telling me what I should and shouldn't do as if I were a child. More than that, I didn't want anyone telling Simon Cowell what to do, because he's got a lot of good singers and he didn't need anyone bothering him.

Frankie, the lad who'd come up to help me in Blackburn when it all blew up at the beginning, suggested I might like to ask a friend to come down.

'What about Lorraine?' he said.

'Lorraine's got her hotel to run,' I reminded him.

Lorraine would hardly be able to drop everything just to keep me company. But on the Thursday evening, when I was leaving the studios after spending the whole day rehearsing, another car drew up and out stepped Lorraine, dressed to the nines as usual, and, even though I'd promised myself I'd cope on my own, I have to say I was very pleased to see her!

It's amazing how quickly human beings adjust to changed circumstances and, when you're in the middle of it, you soon get used to a different routine. It takes someone coming in from outside to show you just how weird your life has become. Lorraine couldn't believe the crowds in the hotel lobby, or the chase to the lifts that had become a way of life for me. When we finally reached my room and shut the door behind us, she went over to open the curtains because it was a fine sunny evening.

'You can't do that!' I stopped her. 'Not unless you want to be snapped by the paparazzi!'

'I can't believe you're living like this!' Lorraine exclaimed.

'I haven't been out since Monday,' I told her. 'Except to the studio.'

'That's not right,' said Lorraine, checking her make-up in the mirror. 'We're in London, so you and I are going to go and have ourselves a wee girls' night out!'

It was one of those summer evenings we don't get enough of in our cold, wet country, where the air remains warm even after the sun has gone down. Tables and chairs appear on the pavement outside pubs and coffee shops, and the whole world seems to be out on the streets making the most of it.

'Look, it's Susan Boyle!'

Everyone we passed stopped us to say hello, and I posed with them so their mate could take a picture on their mobile phone. As cars went past, they were slowing down and tooting their horns. One almost smashed into a taxi cab because he was looking at me, not the road.

Lorraine stood with her mouth open.

'You've had one showing on telly, Susan,' she said, 'but they've never forgot you!'

It took quite a while to walk a couple of hundred yards, and when we finally got up to Wembley High Street, we were trying to find somewhere quiet to eat, but it was mainly McDonald's and Nando's-type places, which are nice, but very public. Then Lorraine spotted a little Greek restaurant. I'd never eaten Greek food before but Lorraine said it was good, so we went in. As soon as we were inside, I noticed two familiar figures sitting at the back of the restaurant –

Yvie and Nigel, the musical director. I didn't think they'd want to be seen with us, so I said to Lorraine, 'We cannae sit in here.'

Lorraine said, 'Well, we cannae go outside now.'

I turned round to see a bank of eager faces smiling at me through the door. It was going to be the same anywhere we went. By that time, Yvie and Nigel had spotted us and they asked us to join them, which was very nice of them, but I didn't feel comfortable because I was very aware that some of the other competitors' families already thought I was getting special treatment.

All the bookies had me down as the winner, and it was me the photographers went after, even though I always suggested they take pictures of the other contestants too. I knew better than anybody else not to believe what everyone said. I had a semi-final to get through before I even got to the final. I also had a long track record of coming second in almost every singing competition I'd ever entered in my life.

Lorraine was right. Greek food is delicious, and I had quite an appetite. Yvie and Nigel finished and left before we did, and over coffee Lorraine said she'd noticed an Irish pub with live music just down the road, so why didn't we go there for a wee drink? However, when we came out of the restaurant, everyone I'd spoken to on the way up to the High Street seemed to have texted their friends and now there were hundreds of people waiting for us. Everyone, whether they were young or old, wanted a piece of me. Don't get me wrong – I am always pleased to meet fans, but it took a very long time to get back to the hotel.

I needed to get a passport photo done, so the next morning Lorraine suggested we try the Asda up the road. We decided not to risk walking and ordered a cab. Dashing from the car into the store, I went into the booth and pulled the curtain across so my face couldn't be seen.

'Don't you move till I get back,' Lorraine whispered. She went off to get a few toiletries that we needed while we waited for the photo to develop.

But when she returned, less than ten minutes later, I'd been surrounded by about thirty lads, all ringing their mates, saying, 'You'll never guess who I'm with!'

We had to order another cab to get back to the hotel, although it wasn't more than a couple of hundred yards. That's when Lorraine said, 'Right. We'll have to stay in the hotel.'

The problem with that was that the weekend of the semi-finals of *Britain's Got Talent* coincided with three Wembley play-offs for promotion from football League Two, League One and Championship. Where were the fans staying? The Wembley Plaza Hotel. So on top of the contestants, their families, the fans and the press, the hotel lobby and bar were now filled with football supporters. If you've ever seen the Marx Brothers' film *A Night at the Opera*, where Groucho is in a cabin on a liner and he keeps ordering more room service, and the tiny space fills up with dozens of waiters and maids and technicians all on top of each other, you'll know how it felt in the lobby of the hotel. Sheer pandemonium!

On the Friday night there were just a few fans who'd made the journey to see Shrewsbury Town play Gillingham. On Saturday the noise increased as the supporters of League One's Scunthorpe came down to face London club Millwall. But on Sunday the place was packed with fans in claret and blue for Burnley, and red and white for Sheffield United, who were lined up against each other in one of football's biggest games, with the winners getting into the Premiership. It didn't bother them that I was a Celtic supporter; they all wanted my autograph just the same.

Breakfast was hectic, and lunch was hectic, so Lorraine said to me, 'Susan, this isn't enjoyable. I think what we should do is go down at half past seven rather than nine o'clock to get our breakfast.'

But half seven was hectic too, so we decided to get our meals in our room.

'I knew I was coming down to help on a famous television programme,' Lorraine joked, as we sat on our twin beds with the curtains drawn. 'But I didn't realize it was going to be *Prisoner Cell Block H*!'

Instead of sleeping, I was lying in bed most of the night with my heart palpitating and my eyes wide open, trying to block out endless choruses of 'We are going up, we are going up!' floating up from the bar. My mood was all over the place. One minute I was cresting along on a wave of giddy excitement, the next I was sinking down into the cold depths of fear. Sunday was the night when I had to show that I wasn't just good for one song, but had a real future as a professional singer. If I made a mess of it, all the interest in me would disappear as instantly as it had arrived. I'd watched enough reality television to know that. Simon Cowell had called it 'the most important performance of my life'. No pressure there, then.

My friends Sadie and Patricia from church came down from Scotland for the weekend to see the semi-final, along with my niece Joanne and her husband Kenny. Kirsty was also there and they all tried to help me relax by offering to take me out for a few hours, but that wasn't possible because I never knew when I was going to be needed for rehearsals. It would have been nice to have a bit of a break in different surroundings, but I didn't want to cause any problems, so again I felt caught in the middle.

The only place I was able to focus on what really mattered was in the rehearsal room. Yvie understands about nerves because she's worked with so many singers, but she doesn't take kindly to crying because it's bad for your voice. We established a routine where Yvie would start singing the exercise and I'd sing it back. As soon as I was singing, none of the stuff that was going on outside mattered. I was exhausted from lack of sleep, but when it came to singing I possessed incredible reserves of stamina.

You could taste the tension in the air, and not just among the performers. The production team, who always appeared so professional with their head-phones and head mics, were a wee bit brittle. Delivering a live television programme was almost as scary for them as it was for us.

Finally, there was no more preparation to be done. The producer of the show had let me get ready in Piers Morgan's dressing room as a special treat. (He wasn't there, of course!) Frock on, hair tamed, face painted, I kept glancing at the mirror, as if to catch it unawares. Wandering up and down the corridor before the show was about to begin, I bumped into Piers on his way to his seat. I had a big crush on him and I thought, 'Oh my God, this is my chance to talk to him in person,' so I said, 'Hi, Piers!'

And he said, 'Whoa! It's you!'

'Yes!'

'People in the States are always asking me, "How is Susan Boyle?"'

'I'm fine, no problems,' I told him.

'Well, I'll see you later,' he said.

I'd finally met another one of my heroes. I was buzzing.

The opening credits of the programme are designed to stoke up the excitement for the audience at home, so you can imagine how thrilling it feels to be backstage. Adrenalin starts coursing through your veins, but that boost is difficult to hang on to, and I was last in the running order, not due to go on for another hour.

It was the longest and the shortest hour of my life. I didn't want to get in anyone's way, so I stayed in my dressing room, but I could hear the applause from the audience after each act. It sounded like a good, supportive audience, and I knew that Lorraine, Patricia and Sadie were out there, as well as Joanne and Kenny, and Kirsty and her husband Shaun. I wanted them to be proud of me. I thought of Bridie tuning in to the show in her flat in Motherwell. At least she'd have no quarrel with the way I looked tonight. Each time I glimpsed myself in the mirror, there was a split second when I thought, 'Who's that?'

Walking to my starting position behind the screens was like wading through treacle. My mind had gone blank. I'd rehearsed my song, practised it in my hotel room and warmed up with Yvie, but now I couldn't remember what note I was supposed to come in on. My mouth was so dry, it was likely no sound would emerge at all. What were the words? I told myself, 'For God's sake, Susan, whatever you do, don't slide down that runway.'

As I waited there, listening to the video-tape introduction, I heard myself on tape saying, 'All my life I've wanted to prove that I'm a worthwhile person . . .'

The stage manager was frowning at me, and I realized that I was pulling funny faces, like you do when you hear yourself talking on tape.

'Susan Boyle!'

The screens parted. I could hear cheering, but I couldn't see the audience because the lights were very bright. I tried not to look at the judges in front of me. I didn't even think about the millions of people out there watching me. All I was thinking about was getting to that microphone in my high bronze shoes without falling over.

The first arpeggios of the backing track started slightly sooner than I expected, I opened my mouth to sing and was suddenly trapped in my worst nightmare. The cold that had been coming on all week made my voice croaky, and the wrong notes came out.

You don't stop, you keep going!

It had been drilled into us at the Edinburgh Acting School all those years ago. Through the mist of dry ice swirling round my feet, I spotted Yvie sitting in her position just next to Piers.

'You can't control your nerves, but you can control your breathing.'

I placed my hand on my diaphragm and, thank God, it worked.

The judges were very generous with their comments. Piers told me that I'd cheered the world up; Amanda said I'd nailed the song, which wasn't true because the first note was bad. Then Simon started apologizing for laughing at the audition and that was embarrassing, so I put on a funny voice and tried to make a joke of it.

'I know nothing, I am from Barcelona.'

It was a reference to the hapless character Manuel in the classic sitcom *Fawlty Towers*, and I was doing my classic thing of being a wee bit off the wall. I realized when Simon looked askance.

'She's not from Barcelona, by the way!' said Dec.

Backstage, the more I looked at the other contestants, the more I wondered how I had ever thought I stood a chance. I'd seen all their acts time and again at rehearsals. Diversity were fantastic dancers and a great bunch of lads. That little Perri, what a character! Ashley Banjo was one of the tallest guys I'd ever encountered, and one of the politest too. Little Natalie had a great voice and she was a cute wee dancer. I was sure the audience at home would like her. Then there was Sue Son, who had a great story, and people liked a modern take on a classical instrument. You just had to think of how well Escala did in the previous series. Faces of Disco had a very entertaining act, something different. To be honest, I wasn't too bothered about Darth Jackson or Nick Hell, but you never knew what the audience would go for.

I was the only one who had messed up.

For the first time, I thought about all the millions of people picking up their phones to vote. I couldn't imagine anybody wanting to vote for me.

It is terrifying standing waiting for the results. You're hoping that they'll call out your name and at the same time you're telling yourself it's not going to happen and you're trying to set your face into a suitably dignified mask that won't show how disappointed you are.

'Susan Boyle!'

Oh my God!

I was so gobsmacked, I literally didn't know which way to turn and started walking the wrong way, until I was called to the other side of the stage by Dec.

I was walking on air, I was dancing on the spot, and then I did what I'd promised myself I would never do again because it's just not what professional singers are supposed to do. The wiggle. Not once, but twice, and another one specially for Piers.

Oh my God!

28

Final

The backlash began almost immediately. People started writing and tweeting their reviews of the semi-final, and some of them weren't exactly complimentary. To be honest, they had a point. I knew better than anyone else that it hadn't been my best performance, but the public had had the opportunity to vote me out and they had kept me in, so there wasn't anything I could do about it.

I tried to avoid the newspapers, but that was no longer possible with everyone asking me for my comments as soon as I stepped out of my room. There were undercover journalists staying in the hotel now. Lorraine and I started to recognize them lurking in the corridors. I tried not to take the criticism personally, but my high spirits came crashing down to earth with a bang.

It was a week since I'd arrived in the Wembley Plaza Hotel, and I was running out of clean clothes to wear because I hadn't expected to stay for the final.

Lorraine had also been planning to return to Scotland, but now the producers of the programme asked her if she would continue to keep me company. It was difficult for her because she had things to arrange at her hotel, but she agreed because she feared for me being on my own. The producers of *Britain's Got Talent* were very sensitive about me being seen to be treated differently from the other contestants, so a secret plan was drawn up whereby Lorraine and I would fly to Scotland, spend Monday night at her partner Benny's house, pick up what we needed, then return the following morning. We made our escape in cars with tinted windows and managed to get through the airport unnoticed. We can laugh about it now, but when you're in the middle of the subterfuge you feel as if you've done something wrong, like a criminal on the run.

Benny met us at the other end and drove us to his house. Once we had checked that there were no paparazzi lurking, I managed to nip into Yule Terrace to get some clothes and things I needed. The house sounded a wee bit echoey with nobody there, but it was fantastic to feel the familiar texture of the banister, the carpet, the sofa in the back room, and to see all the pictures and ornaments, each with its own memory, that made it my home. I knew I had to be quick, because if anyone spotted me news would travel fast, but as I stood in the back room, gazing at the little figure of Our Lady in the corner, I paused for a moment. What if I just stayed behind? Lorraine would be able to return to her work and I could get my old life with Pebbles back.

I thought about my mum sitting in her chair. What would she say if she were here in the room with me now?

'You're not going to let a couple of bad reviews stop you, are you, Susan? Thousands of people have spent good money voting for you. You can't let them down!'

My fighting mood returned. I'd show everyone I could do better. I would! I'd show them!

Burnley had been promoted to the Premiership and their supporters had left to celebrate back at home. The hotel lobby was quieter.

'Do you fancy a cup of tea?' Lorraine suggested, walking ahead of me towards the bar.

When I failed to answer, she turned round and saw that I'd been swallowed into the middle of a Japanese television crew. They were all smiling expectantly, bowing and speaking to me in Japanese, but I had no idea what they were asking. It sounded like 'Blaa blaa blaa, Susan Boyle, blaa blaa blaa, Susan Boyle . . .'

One of the men was filming my face with a hand-held camera, another was wielding a great big furry mic on a pole, another was holding a mic to my face, and there were about twenty others bobbing around me.

Lorraine said, 'Susan, let's forget about the tea and go up to the room.'

I was trying to be polite, bowing back to them as they bowed to me, which only made them bow and smile even more.

'Blaa blaa, Susan Boyle, blaa blaa, Susan Boyle!'

'Thank you, thank you!'

I felt like the Queen, but what else was I supposed to say?

Lorraine started frantically pushing the buttons to try to call the lifts, while the Japanese were grabbing at me, urgently, as if they were trying to tell me something important.

The lifts weren't arriving.

'Quick, let's go up the stairs!' Lorraine suggested, flying towards the fire exit and straight into the furry mic, which is actually not as soft as it looks.

'Blaa blaa, Susan Boyle, blaa blaa, Susan Boyle!'

'Are you all right, Lorraine?' I called over the crowd.

'I'm fine, Susan,' called Lorraine, but she was rubbing her head. 'What are we going to do?'

The Japanese woman who was holding the mic in front of my face finally mustered the language to say, 'Future husband!'

An ancient Japanese man I hadn't noticed was thrust in front of me.

'You kiss future husband!'

The old guy went to put his arms around me to

give me a kiss. He must have been at least eighty years old!

'Hell, no way!' I said.

Of all the stupid things I've said, the one that's caused me most bother is my remark about never having been kissed. As I made clear at the time, it was not an advert, but nobody ever remembers that bit.

When we finally made it back to our darkened room, Lorraine and I both fell on to our beds laughing, but it was the last time we'd do that for a while, because if the pressure had been difficult to handle until then, it was nothing compared to the week that was to come.

That evening, along with some of the other contestants, we watched the third live semi-final on the big screen in the hotel bar. I was constantly being pestered by journalists, so I left before the end of the programme.

The following morning, the front pages of the tabloids had the story that I had sworn at the television in the bar downstairs and flicked a V sign at the screen following Piers's comments about Shaheen's performance. All I can tell you is that if I did make such a gesture, it was only as a kind of 'Go on with you! I thought you said you liked me!' kind of joke. I would never, ever criticize a fellow singer.

Reading the reports was like freefalling into a dark chasm. I'd never believed in the fairy story. I'd always half expected a note saying, 'Ha ha, only kidding!' But nothing had prepared me for being turned into an ugly monster.

I didn't feel safe any more. I was terrified to leave my room until we got a call that the car was outside the hotel, and then Lorraine and I would make a dash for it. On one occasion I made the mistake of waiting while Lorraine went to get a bottle of water for me. A woman approached and asked if I would have my photo taken with a girl in a wheelchair, so of course I agreed. But when Lorraine returned she noticed the girl was very agitated, then the girl's mother came up and pushed the wheelchair away. I'd assumed that the first woman who'd asked for the photo was the mother, but she wasn't, she was a journalist.

Lorraine said, 'How dare you? I can't believe you've just done that!'

The journalist asked me, cool as you like, 'Is it true you were shouting at Piers Morgan on the television?'

I just snapped. I went ballistic.

And the journalist said, 'Well, you've just proved my point!' and walked out smirking.

I know the press have their job to do, but when they start trying to create stories using a disabled person as a prop, I think that oversteps the line of decency.

'That's it!' said Lorraine. 'I want the police involved here. I'm sick and tired of people trying to set you up!'

And so the police got involved, and that led to more stories in the papers about me losing the plot.

'Boyling Point!' screamed the headlines above reports about me shouting. Nobody reported what had happened just before.

I'd entered a television talent show, so I'd put myself in the arena, but I never claimed to be perfect. All I wanted to do was sing. I couldn't understand how I'd suddenly become Public Enemy Number One. People try to tell you that today's newsprint is tomorrow's litter-tray liner, but they don't know what it's like when you're the one portrayed, and if you complain, you only make things worse. I felt the same humiliating powerlessness as I had in the playground at school when people were saying nasty things about me. I couldn't stop crying.

My dream of success and independence was crashing down around my head. I thought my only hope was to go back home, shut my door and try to pick up the pieces of my life, so I packed my case and phoned the producer to tell her I was quitting. She suggested that I have a chat to Piers Morgan, so he came on the phone and I tried to explain through my tears what had been happening.

He was very honest, actually, because he said he had been a journalist himself once, and he had chased people. If I gave up now, I'd be doing exactly what the press wanted me to do. He advised me to go back and prove my point. I should say to myself, and to them, non-verbally, obviously, 'I'm going to go through with this and to hell with you!'

'Should I leave my cases where they are, then?' I sniffed.

'Yes,' he said.

The next day, there was a torrent of stories and speculation about whether I was staying or going. It all added to the strain of rehearsing all day, sometimes until late at night. All the fuss around me wasn't really helping the other finalists, who were all under a lot of stress themselves. But some of them, particularly Stavros Flatley, Diversity, Flawless and wee Aidan's mum, are very grounded people and they were very supportive to me.

After a great deal of debate, Lorraine and I were finally allowed to leave the Wembley hotel to go to stay in a house in Chelsea with a lovely woman who is a cousin of Benny's. A secret location, it said in the papers.

Still I couldn't sleep. I was awake throughout the night, listening to the rumble of the teeming city that's never perfectly quiet even in the small hours of the morning. I must have drifted off around dawn, waking up again only a couple of hours later in unfamiliar surroundings and taking a moment to remember where I was. Chelsea. It wasn't an area I knew at all, but I was so desperate to get outside in the air that I decided to go out for a walk.

Closing the heavy front door behind me carefully so as not to disturb anyone, I stepped out into the street. The house was on a busy through road, and there was a strong smell of exhaust as cars and buses thundered past, but it was great to be outside. I hadn't seen the sky for so long, it was exhilarating to look up at the sheer expanse of blue dotted with just a few cotton-wool clouds.

Glancing left and right along the tree-lined street, I didn't know what I was going to do or where I was going. I decided to head off towards the junction I could see in the distance where the street I was on crossed a main road. I thought I might find a newsagent and buy a paper to see what they were saying about me today. As I started walking, I felt very happy to be outside, and a wee bit naughty, almost like I was sneaking off early from school.

At the crossroads, I turned left and headed towards a Tesco Express sign a hundred yards or so along the road.

Back at the house, the housekeeper had seen me leave, and she rushed up to Lorraine, who had only just got up and was in the shower.

'Madam! Madam! Susan's left!'

'What?' Lorraine came out of the shower, pulled on her jeans and T-shirt and ran out in her slippers. She could just see me at the end of the street, about to turn into the main road. She raced after me, calling, 'Susan!'

I turned round impatiently but I didn't stop walking.

'I just want to walk down the street. OK?' I said, irritated, when Lorraine caught me up.

'Well, you cannae!' she protested, panting from her run. 'You're too big now just to walk down the street!'

'I just want to get a newspaper!' I said, shrugging her off, and marching into the Tesco Express.

Sure enough, my face was all over the *Sun* and the *Mirror*. I bought a copy of each and scanned the stories.

'Come on, Susan!' Lorraine was hissing at me, aware that I was beginning to attract attention. People in the shop had obviously recognized me and, as we went back out on the street, cars were slowing to have a look at me.

'Let's go back, then,' I said.

'We cannae go back now,' Lorraine cried, exasperated. 'They'll follow us and it's meant to be a secret location!'

She looked around desperately, trying to work out what to do. I noticed that she was still wearing her slippers.

The crowd was growing now. The traffic on the main road was very loud and getting louder because, as people saw it was me, they were beeping their horns and winding down their windows to shout out 'Good luck!'

We were standing outside a funeral director's. Next

door was an estate agent's. There wasn't even a café we could duck into. Further up the road there was a big hospital, but I didn't want to go in there and cause a commotion. We were trapped.

I don't know what made us both look up at that moment and find ourselves staring at a statue of Jesus above the words 'Servite Catholic Church'. A church entrance seemed completely incongruous right in the middle of an ordinary terrace of shops. It didn't look like any other church I'd ever seen, but it appeared that we were standing outside Our Lady of Dolours Catholic Church. You could walk past it a hundred times without noticing.

The iron gates to the small, arched vestibule were open, but the glass door into the church was firmly closed. We read the Mass times. Morning Mass was at ten o'clock and there wasn't another until 6.30 in the evening. With so little sleep, I was finding it difficult to keep track of time, but I think it must have been around midday.

Lorraine spotted an entry-phone on the side wall. It looked so old, I doubted it would work, but Lorraine pressed the buzzer anyway.

'Can I help you?'

It was difficult to hear the voice because of the traffic noise outside.

'Can you let us in, please?' said Lorraine.

'I'm sorry, the church is closed, I'm afraid,' said the woman's voice.

'But I'm desperate,' said Lorraine. 'I've got Susan Boyle here.'

'You're having me on,' said the voice.

'No, I'm not joking!'

In fact, Lorraine was on the brink of tears.

'Wait, I'll come down,' said the voice.

A moment or two later, a very pretty lady appeared.

'Oh my goodness,' she said. 'It *is* Susan Boyle!'

And she opened the door into the colonnade inside that leads to the door of the church. There were a few tables and chairs there, and all the parish notices pinned up on noticeboards.

'Would you believe all the things they're saying about me in the press,' I thrust the papers at the nice lady. 'It's not true, you know!'

'You don't have to pay to read that and give yourself pain,' she replied soothingly. 'You don't need to explain to me. Those are just gossip-mongers. There are millions of people out there who love you. I can tell you that.'

She told us she was the parish secretary, then sat us down on the chairs and went to get the parish priest, who was having his lunch.

'I've got Susan Boyle here,' she said.

'You're joking!' he said.

'I'm not,' she told him. 'And I'd really appreciate it if you could have a word, because she's very upset.'

So Father Dermot came down to meet us.

'Would you like to see inside the church?' he asked.

'I would,' I told him.

Father Dermot and I went on a tour of the church, while Lorraine went upstairs with the lady for a cup of tea.

It is the sort of old church that you would expect to find standing alone in some prominent position in a town, surrounded by a churchyard, so it felt very strange that instead it was almost hidden on a busy London street. As Father Dermot opened the glass door and we stepped inside the cool, dim interior with its dark stone columns and high vaulted ceiling, it felt as surprising and magical as finding Narnia at the back of a wardrobe.

The priest told me a little about the history of the place and pointed out the stone pietà, with Our Lady cradling Christ's body. In front of it, there was a special prayer in a frame, handwritten and decorated like a manuscript. Some of the words seemed particularly resonant for me at that time: 'Take and offer on the Cross our labours, weariness and low spirits and struggles and faint-heartedness . . .'

Murmuring those words before a representation of such courage, I was able to put my own struggles into perspective. As often happens in church, I came away feeling much lighter and refreshed.

Upstairs in the Founders Room, the lady, whose name was Dupe, had made a cup of tea and offered me one of my favourite ginger biscuits. Lorraine had cheered herself up and we were all feeling much better.

'Dupe – that's not a name I've heard before,' I said.

'I come from Nigeria,' Dupe told me. 'All African names have meaning. My full name is much longer, and it means "Thank God", but Dupe is the short version.'

'Are you going to give us a song now, Susan?' asked Father Dermot.

His Irish accent made me feel completely at home. So I sang 'The Fields of Athenry', which is an old Irish ballad that dates from the famine, but is probably better known as the anthem of the Celtic supporters. Father Dermot and Lorraine joined in the chorus.

By the time we left an hour or so later, we were feeling much more relaxed. As we said goodbye, I left the newspapers behind with Dupe.

'We are one hundred per cent behind you,' she said. 'And I can assure you of the prayers of this parish.'

'I'm sure there's a reason for this, Susan,' Lorraine said, in the cab back to the house. 'I don't know the reason, but there is a reason and it will make you survive this, because you give the world something good.'

It was a nice thought to take back with me to the studios for the final rehearsals that carried on all that day, until after midnight.

* * *

The stories in the newspapers I had read that morning had turned to criticism of the programme. That had made everyone jumpy and upped the tension all around me. The producers were getting nervous. My family were worried. Simon Cowell spoke to me himself and told me that if I didn't want to do the show, then I didn't have to. But I did want to do the show. It was the opportunity I'd been waiting for all my life. So that was that, but still I couldn't seem to stop all the noise and arguments and images flashing around my head.

Lorraine had been hanging around Wembley all day waiting for me and when we finally got into the car to go back to Chelsea, we were both exhausted.

It didn't help that the paparazzi saw me get into the car and started to give chase.

The driver said, 'I'll see if I can get away from them.'

So he put his foot down and we were thrown back in our seats. I was looking through the front windscreen at how close he was getting to the cars in front, my knuckles gripping the seat as he swerved out to overtake. We were jumping red lights, and in the end I was so scared I just closed my eyes and prayed. Next to me, Lorraine was looking out of the back window, doing a running commentary in my ear. We weren't losing them, and she was panicking because she had done her best to get me to a place where I could be myself and relax, but now there were guys on motor-bikes chasing us with cameras.

'I don't know what I'm going to do,' the driver said. 'They're determined.'

Lorraine got out her phone and rang the people we were staying with, and she was saying, 'They're going to cause an accident! It's like Princess Diana here!'

That didn't exactly help me calm down, so I shouted at her, 'For God's sake, Lorraine!'

And she screamed back, 'It's not my fault, Susan! It's out of my control!'

When we finally arrived outside the house in Chelsea, Lorraine said, 'We can't get out of the car. We'll have to get the police.'

She was seeing them as a physical threat, as if it were guns not cameras they were pointing. I was all for getting out and giving them what they wanted, but she wouldn't let me. So now the two of us were going at each other like a couple of headless chickens.

The driver told Lorraine that there was nothing the police could do if the paparazzi didn't touch us, so we had to get out and run the gauntlet.

'I've taken a lot of celebrities,' he said, 'but I've never had anything like this. You're big, Susan!'

'I'm only five foot three,' I told him.

In those sort of circumstances, you have to keep your sense of humour.

* * *

That night, I sat on the chaise longue staring at nothing. My brain was whirling inside my head like a waltzer at a fairground.

In less than twenty hours I was going to have to get out there and sing live on television to an estimated audience of twenty million people and the car was coming for me at seven o'clock in the morning. I didn't get one single second of sleep.

I'd never seen so many flowers. There were more flowers than in a florist's shop, at least a hundred bouquets, and that was first thing in the morning. Flowers kept arriving all day and the scent was heavenly. I was so overwhelmed I burst into tears. People from all over the world were wishing me well – film stars, politicians, football teams, as well as names I didn't recognize. There were presents too, scarves and lucky charms. Lorraine and I started reading each of the labels and we should have written down a list, but I was so busy there wasn't time. I'll take this opportunity to say a long overdue thank-you to everyone who was so generous.

To say that I was wobbly on the day of the final would be an understatement. I tried to eat a wee bit of breakfast, and a bed was put in my dressing room, but I still couldn't rest, and the nerves were beginning to build again.

I'd assumed that nerves would be something you'd get used to. After the semi-final I'd thought nothing could be worse than that. I'd sung on live television and I hadn't done as well as I could have, but I'd survived. Weren't nerves all about fear of the unknown? But since then I'd had virtually no sleep, I hadn't eaten properly for days, and the world had turned against me. The stakes seemed higher than ever.

I was called in with Lorraine to see Simon Cowell.

He asked me if I could remember what I said at my first audition.

'I'm going to go out there and make that audience rock!' I told him, through my tears.

'Well, get out there and do it!' he said.

I came out of his office feeling resolved. There was no going back. But that still didn't make the nerves go away.

The song I was singing was 'I Dreamed a Dream'. I started thinking that if I messed up, the clip would fly round the world just like last time and that would be it for me. The newspapers were probably writing the headlines already: 'Fallen Angel!' I didn't want to let my family down, nor all the people in Blackburn and the rest of the world who had supported me.

Lorraine had an idea.

'Let's ring Frank Quinn,' she said. 'If anyone can calm you down, it's him.'

Poor Frank was on a weekend away with his wife and some friends of theirs in Lytham St Annes, and I expect the last thing he wanted was me weeping down the phone. But as usual, his calm reassurance helped me see through all my worries.

'Susan,' he said, 'the result of this thing does not matter. What matters is that you are given the opportunity to stand up there and sing.'

I could tell that the production team were losing patience with me. My outbursts were becoming a nuisance. Lorraine was doing her best to soothe me but, as you do with the people you know best, I was kicking off at her as well. The programme-makers decided that her presence wasn't helping, so Lorraine was sent off to the canteen to get some lunch. The way things turned out, I didn't see her again for several weeks.

In my dressing room, I was climbing the walls. Every time I calmed down enough for the hair and make-up people to come in, they'd put the make-up on my face and I'd wash it all off with my tears. There was mascara pouring down my cheeks and when I looked in the mirror, the face that looked back was ragged and miserable, as if I had turned into the ugly character the papers were writing about.

In my warm-up with Yvie we went through the Vvvvvvvs, the kitten, the lot. Yvie started singing and I sang back, just as we always did in our lessons. The regular breathing and the familiar rhythms grabbed hold of my racing heart and my whirling brain and slowed them down.

Yvie was conscious that I was tired, but when she asked me, 'Would you like to go over the song again?' I said yes please. I didn't seem to be tired when I was singing.

'It really is a natural thing for you,' Yvie told me. 'When you're singing, you're fine. You'll be fine once you get out there and sing.'

So there I was, sitting in my long, shimmery gown. My make-up had been done for the final time. The show was on air, but I was way down the running order, eighth in a list of ten. I wasn't aware of what was happening with the other acts. I wasn't aware of anything except that time was running out for me.

I can't do it! I can't do it!

In desperation, I rang Frank Quinn again. We said a prayer together, and just before stepping out in front of an audience of millions, I found the quiet place that is my faith.

'Now, Susan,' he told me, 'when you go out there, on your right hand will be Our Lady and on your left hand will be your mother. You are in the middle, and you've got the job of singing.'

29

Aftermath

Somehow I got myself out on that stage. Somehow I sang. Somehow I remembered to thank everyone who had supported me.

'That's where you really feel at home, isn't it, on stage?' Ant asked me.

'I really feel at home on stage,' I told him, truthfully. 'I am among friends, am I not?' I wasn't so sure about that last bit.

In the audience, my family were shocked at how I looked. Knowing me so well, they could see the build-up of stress written across my face. Those of them who had been at the semi-final the previous week sensed a colder atmosphere in the audience and that brought out all their protective instincts. You know how families are. They know all your faults, but they'll defend you till the last.

Piers Morgan was the judge who went first and he was very supportive, but when he said that I should win the competition I heard something I'd never had before after a performance. Booing. It was only a few people, but once you've heard the boos, you don't hear the applause any more. It's like being punched. It knocks you off balance. When I looked at a video tape of the final, weeks afterwards, I saw Simon Cowell say that he adored me, but I wasn't aware of that at the time.

Then there was the wait. To be honest, I was so ragged I didn't even know what I felt any more. I forgot what I was supposed to do when my name was called as being in the final three and wandered down to the front of the stage. When Julian the saxophonist was called, he gently guided me to where I was supposed to be. Then it was his turn to leave.

So I was down to the last two.

'And the winner of *Britain's Got Talent* is . . .'

The wait was seventeen seconds.

'Diversity!'

My immediate response was relief. It was over!

My second feeling was genuine pleasure for Diversity, because it was really touching to see great big lads like that crying with happiness. You couldn't wish for a nicer bunch of people. They were fantastic dancers who'd put a lot of work into their act and a bit of humour as well. They deserved to win and I'm glad that I managed to say so, because you really don't know what you're saying out there.

I ended my *Britain's Got Talent* journey as I'd started it. With a wiggle.

So that was that then, I thought as I came off stage. I'd come second. The story of my life. It had been since the very first competition I'd entered, when I'd sung 'Ye Banks and Braes', and the whole school had heard me over the tannoy. Well, it was better than being last, wasn't it?

It was only when I got back to my dressing room that the reality hit me. All those flowers. For nothing! All the humiliation. For nothing! I pulled off my slate-grey shimmery dress and threw it over a chair. The fabric winked at me like a tawdry glitter ball. It wasn't fair!

All the stress that had built up inside me suddenly blew.

'Are you OK?'

'Of course I'm not OK!'

My family were there trying to console me, people from Syco – Simon Cowell's record label – were trying to reassure me. They were all saying it didn't matter. But it did bloody matter. It mattered missing the chance to perform for the Queen. It mattered a hundred thousand pounds, for God's sake! All my expenses had been paid while I was in London, but I'd spent more money than my usual budget over the past weeks. I'd needed new clothes, a haircut, a mobile phone. On top of everything else, I was now going to be in debt.

Everybody was saying different things about what

would happen and what should happen. My family were suggesting that I should go back home and get some rest. The people from Syco were trying to tell me that I could still have a recording contract, but I was exhausted and I needed to get myself well enough. All around me different voices were firing off. Everybody was just diving into the pool, and all the water was going out, and there I was left in the empty shell in my bathing suit.

I wanted so badly to become a professional singer, and now it was all slipping out of my grasp.

My family knew me well enough to realize that the best thing for them to do at this stage was to go and leave my disappointment to burn itself out. It was agreed that I would be taken to a different hotel. Everybody knew that there were press waiting outside the building, and I wasn't looking my best, so one of my nieces picked up one of the bouquets and tried to hide my stricken face behind it. Flowers whose purpose had been to celebrate and wish me well were now being used to hide me.

30

Priory

I regret now that I said that I'd needed to be in the Priory 'for a rest'. I did need a rest, but that wasn't the right place for me.

I was very upset and exhausted the day after the final of *Britain's Got Talent*. I'd had little sleep for a week, but all the adrenalin and emotion after the show still seemed to be pumping round my body, keeping me awake all night. I don't think it helped that I was in a different hotel room, surrounded by strangers. When it was suggested to me that I should go to the Priory, I went along with it because I didn't know what else to do.

I didn't know what the Priory was, but when I arrived I was immediately aware that it was some kind of mental hospital. I found that very frightening because I knew what happened in mental institutions. They locked you up. My uncle Michael had been locked away for years. All the potential he had in life had been taken away from him because by the time he came out to live with us, he was too old and too traumatized to lead a full life.

I wasn't mental. I tried to explain that to the doctors, but they didn't seem to want to know.

I wanted to phone out, but they wouldn't let me. I wasn't allowed to see a television either, so I didn't know that my story was being followed in the news. I didn't even know if anyone knew I was there. I thought I was locked up and they were going to keep me indefinitely. It was the most terrifying thing that has ever happened to me in my entire life.

I was still trying to accept that my dream was over, but this was truly a nightmare, on a completely different level from being chased by the paparazzi or vilified in the newspapers. I felt as if I was having to fight for my survival as a person, literally to fight for my sanity.

I have never felt more alone, because I couldn't get in touch with anyone who could help me. I wished my mother was there. I knew what she would say was, 'This is not right. This is not the place for Susan.'

But she wasn't there.

When I was finally allowed to use the phone, I called the first telephone number in my memory, which was my sister Kathleen's house.

My niece Pamela answered the phone.

'They've put me in here and it's a mental home,' I told her.

'Susan, it's the Priory,' said Pamela. 'All the stars go there. Have you not seen anybody famous yet?'

'It's not funny,' I told her.

I think she thought, as other people do, that the Priory is like a kind of spa for celebrities to relax in. But it's not.

When nurses came into my room, I was saying, 'Get away! I don't need you!', but it was starting to dawn on me that the angrier I was, the more they thought there was something wrong with me. The best thing to do was to keep quiet.

On the third day, I left.

As the car pulled out of the Priory, with a Chinese driver wearing dark glasses in the front and me in the back with a bodyguard, the paparazzi followed, so we went into an underground garage and I changed cars. The paps followed an empty car. If I'd felt as if I was the central character in a psychological thriller, now I was in a James Bond movie.

We drove to a place on the outskirts of London which had once been a convent but had been converted into luxury houses. I was finally able to get some rest.

After a couple of days, a glamorous doctor came to take me out to a boutique for 'shopping therapy'. The press were there to witness my recovery. At least that proved that I was right and there was nothing wrong with me apart from exhaustion.

So there you are.

Part Four

Who I Was
Born to Be

31

Ave Maria

August 2009

There were golden, late-summer roses in the front garden of St Bennet's, a large Victorian house in the Morningside district of Edinburgh, where His Eminence Cardinal Keith Patrick O'Brien resides. In the corner of the garden facing the entrance, as if welcoming us there, stood a statue of Our Lady. The car tyres swished to a standstill on the gravel drive. As soon as I got out, I immediately sensed the tranquillity of the place. I walked along the path of flagstones that led to the statue and said a prayer, as I always have done since I was a wee girl and my mother taught me how.

The inscription over the front door of the house reads 'SALVA ME BONA CRUX', meaning 'Save me, good Cross'.

Frank and his wife Maureen were there, along with Mario Marzella of the musical West Lothian family, Lorraine, Benny and Sadie. Frank and Mario already knew the Cardinal well from their work at St Joseph's, but for the rest of us it was very exciting to be there and some of us were a wee bit nervous as we waited for the bell to be answered. As devout Catholics, an invitation to lunch with a cardinal of the Catholic Church was an honour and a privilege none of us had ever dreamed of.

The door was opened by Norah, the Cardinal's assistant. A lovely, Irish-looking lady with red hair and a sparkling smile, she immediately put us at ease as she showed us into the reception hall where His Eminence was waiting below the statue of St Andrew, the patron saint of Scotland. His Eminence greeted us all individually and said that it was wonderful to welcome me and my friends to his home. We then followed him along the corridor to the private oratory.

St Bennett's was originally owned by a solicitor and was bought from him by the Catholic Church in 1878, so the corridor is fairly dark, just like any other big Victorian dwelling, with carpet underfoot and closed doors leading off. The oratory was added to the building about a hundred years ago and nothing prepared us for the beauty that was revealed when the door to it was opened. Those of us who had not been there before gasped as we walked in. It is a perfect miniature jewel of a chapel, with rose pink walls, white stucco columns and bright stained-glass windows that flood the interior with intense light. On the left of the altar is a statue of St Joseph, and on the right is a very delicate statue of Our Lady looking young and ethereal, with her robes floating around her. It was an incredibly beautiful and uplifting place in which to celebrate the Mass of the Assumption together.

The Cardinal in his robes is a figure of immense power and authority. After Mass, he asked me if I would like to sing in the chapel, but I felt far too awed, and overcome with shyness.

A photographer had arrived to record our visit and I was allowed to sit on a chair made specially for Pope John Paul II when he visited Scotland all those years ago. I remembered so clearly bowing to him as he passed by me on the Mound in his white Popemobile. Sitting in his chair, in a chapel he had prayed in, it almost felt as if my life had come full circle.

We all went to the dining room for our lunch. I was seated opposite the Cardinal and I felt tongue-tied at first, but he soon put me at my ease because he's a very approachable man with a twinkly smile and a great sense of humour.

After the final of *Britain's Got Talent*, His Eminence had sent me a second card congratulating me on my achievement, and he'd obviously kept up to date with the reports in the press since then. As we ate, he told me that wherever he went in the world, when he said he was from Scotland people always asked, 'Do you know Susan Boyle? How is Susan Boyle?'

When he'd been in Ireland recently, President Mary McAleese had told him that all the generations of her whole family had come together to watch me in the final. She'd made a meal, and it was the first time they'd had an evening together for a long time. My singing brought people together.

'Saturday-night entertainment's always done that,' I said, not wanting to take the credit.

The Cardinal asked me about the journey that I'd been on over the past few months. I told him that I'd had my ups and downs, but that things seemed to be falling into place now. I was recording an album and I wasn't allowed to say anything about it, but I wanted him to know that there would be hymns included. He was pleased about that and said he hoped I'd give him a copy when it was released. I said I certainly would. I couldn't believe how easy it was to talk to him.

Afterwards, we went back to his comfortable sitting room for coffee. In our living room at home there are all sorts of religious statues and souvenirs from shrines we've visited, so I was surprised to see there was no religious imagery at all in the Cardinal's sitting room, although clearly visible through the large windows there was another stone statue of Our Lady in the leafy back garden. On the mantelpiece there were lots of photos, just like you'd get in any ordinary person's house, except that instead of being of weddings or first communions and occasions like that, these were mementoes of significant moments in the Cardinal's life, like when he was created a cardinal by Pope John Paul II, or one taken in the Sistine Chapel when he was a member of the convocation of cardinals that elected Pope Benedict XVI.

I was relaxed enough to ask him questions about all the photographs, as well as the very large oil painting above the mantelpiece. It is a picture of four French peasant women, one with a baby in her arms, all waiting for their fishermen husbands to return from the sea. To me, it seemed a very human picture rather than the more traditional Christian art you might expect in a cardinal's home. His Eminence told me that it had been given to his predecessor by a friend who was dying, because it was so big he didn't know anyone else who would be able to display it.

'Do you like it?' he asked me.

'I find the expressions on their faces very moving,' I said.

I could tell the women were anxious, not knowing what the future held for them.

The Cardinal smiled at me. I may not be much of an art critic, but I think he knew what I meant.

Before leaving, we all returned to the beautiful little chapel to say prayers together. Now that our nerves had vanished and we were all very comfortable in the Cardinal's company, a profound sense of peace settled over our contemplation. I felt so privileged and so very blessed, I was filled with an unquenchable urge to express my gratitude. While the others remained kneeling, I rose to my feet and, standing in front of the statue of Our Lady, I sang 'Ave Maria'.

My voice sounded as pure and true as sunlight filling the chapel.

Afterwards, there were a few seconds of stillness as the notes remained in the air like the memory of an echo.

The Cardinal thanked me and said that it had been a beautiful and moving moment.

On the way home I was very quiet in the back of the car as I reflected on the day. Of all the amazing times I have enjoyed, this was the one where I most wished my beloved mother could have been present. I know she would have liked the Cardinal. He is such a down-to-earth kind of guy. You can have a laugh with him, and that would have delighted her.

My mother was there spiritually. I'd come to believe that very strongly over recent weeks. In moments of greatest difficulty, I could almost feel her watchful concern, as if she were trying to guide me as she always had. Because she couldn't be there, she was putting the right people in my path. Whenever I had problems, the right person seemed to come along to help me. I was sure she was the reason I had managed to come through the difficult times, and she was with me, too, on wonderful days like today.

32

Andy

After a few days' rest in June, I had been able to rehearse again and join the *Britain's Got Talent* Tour. It was great singing live without the pressure of three buzzers over your head and the atmosphere was completely different from the shows in the television studios. Some of the stadiums we played were huge, like Wembley Arena, which holds six thousand people, and everybody who'd bought tickets to see the tour was out for a good time, not to judge or to criticize, but to enjoy. The noise and excitement rising from the audience was incredible, like waves of energy that you could channel into your performance. It buoyed me up and I got a real buzz from it.

Behind the scenes, though, there was still a lot of confusion about what sort of career I was going to be able to have, and a couple of times the stress built up again so much that I was too tired to perform. I was proud that I managed to sing most nights of the tour, especially in Scotland, where we performed in

Glasgow and Edinburgh, and in Northern Ireland, where my mother's family came from, where we did a show in Belfast. The response from those audiences was fantastic.

Backstage, there was a good atmosphere now that the pressure was off and each of the talented finalists was taking their place in the spotlight. I think my favourite act was Hollie Steel. She's such a wee lassie, with a huge, grown-up voice, and I really enjoyed listening to her singing. But the rest of them were great too.

There was a very sad day halfway through the tour when we learned of the death of Michael Jackson. We were in Bournemouth that evening, in the conference centre that looks out over the sea. It was lovely sunny weather, but inside the mood was dark and very flat. Michael Jackson had been the inspiration for many of the lads, and they were young enough for him to be the first person they'd felt close to who had died. They were wandering around in shock, like zombies. It was extraordinary realizing how much of the show was due to the legendary performer, from the eccentric semi-finalist Darth Jackson to the dance crews Diversity and Flawless, as well as wee Aidan the break-dancer. It was a Michael Jackson song that Shaheen sang in the show, and it was rumoured that Michael Jackson had asked him to be in his upcoming tour, This Is It. Tragically, he only got to sing for Michael Jackson at his funeral.

I don't suppose any of those street-dancing boys thought that, behind the dressing-room door with 'Susan Boyle' written on it, a middle-aged woman who couldn't moonwalk to save her life was weeping too. One of my favourite songs of all time had been Michael Jackson's 'Ben', and I remembered so clearly singing it into my hairbrush with all the heartfelt emotion of a teenager.

That evening we dedicated the show to Michael Jackson, who had given us all so much inspiration.

The *Britain's Got Talent* Tour was very cleverly designed to allow all the finalists a chance to shine in front of their fans, and there were also one or two surprises for the audience. One hilarious moment was the appearance of Darth Jackson, followed on stage by a group of very fit-looking *Star Wars* storm-troopers – the dance crew Flawless dressed up in the white uniforms of the Empire's army. Behind them stomped a couple of shorter, bulkier stormtroopers. It took the audience only a second to realize that the two tagging on at the end were Demi and Lagi, aka Stavros Flatley. That number invariably brought the house down.

Back in London, in my temporary home, my niece Kirsty introduced me to a tall, middle-aged man with something of the look of Harrison Ford himself. To continue with the *Star Wars* theme, his character turned out to be less Han Solo and more Obi-Wan

Kenobi, because he has the patience of a Jedi Master! The man's name was Andy Stephens.

After a lot of discussion, I had decided that my career would be best managed by a team that included Ossie Kilkenny, a management supremo with a great deal of experience, and Kirsty, who is a media lawyer. Between them they could help me navigate through the maze of business relationships and contracts that go on in the background of a music career. It's a complex world and I was very relieved to have people I could trust involved so that I could get on with the singing. A third member of the team, a manager who would look after me on a day-to-day basis, was probably the most important piece of the jigsaw, and that's where Andy Stephens came in. Ossie asked him if he would like to meet me to see if we had the right chemistry.

At the time, I'd only recently been through the very traumatic experience of the Priory and I was in no mood to trust anyone. When Kirsty introduced Andy to me, I was so shy I couldn't look him in the eye.

'I'm not going to hurt you,' he said. 'I just want to have a conversation with you.'

I found him very pleasant and very nice.

A few days later, he took us out to dinner. He talked about his own management experience and how he saw my career progressing, and everything he said seemed to make sense. He didn't want me to rush about doing live concerts all over the place to capitalize on my immediate fame; he wanted to concentrate on getting an album made and then take everything gradually from there, building up in increments to allow me to cope with each different stage. Baby steps, in other words. I found this approach very reassuring.

In an attempt to give me some rest away from the constant intrusion of the press, I had been living in the secluded convent house in North London with a personal assistant, Julia, who had been appointed by the record company. She was staying with me, and I also had a security guy called Ciaran. It was a very luxurious new conversion, but there were no home comforts or things I was familiar with, so it felt a bit like living in a show home. Whenever I went out for a walk in the grounds, I was accompanied. Sometimes you just want to be on your own! I think that the record company must have felt some responsibility to protect me from the press and that's the way they decided to do it, but for someone down to earth like me it was impossible to understand why I couldn't have the same life as before. I missed being with people who knew me in Blackburn. At times, it felt more like being in prison than in a luxury house.

When I met Andy, I instinctively felt that he would be able to help me find a bit of balance, that he would be at my side and, more importantly, on my side. I'm very glad to say that those instincts were to prove correct.

33

Album

If you'd told me when I auditioned in January that six months later I would be recording an album for Simon Cowell's record label, Syco, I would have laughed my head off. Nothing that had happened in the meantime had truly convinced me that the prospect was anything more than another dream. The foundations on which success might be built seemed constantly to be shifting and I never felt as if I was standing on firm ground. Then when Yvie Burnett got back in touch and said that she'd been asked to help me learn the songs for an album, I allowed myself to start believing that it might really be going to happen.

Yvie invited me to come and stay at her house for the time that we were working together. Over break-fast each morning we would decide what songs we were doing that day. We learned one in the morning from ten until twelve, took a wee break for lunch, then went straight back to work on another song from one until five. In the evening we might go over the first song again. Each song required a different placement of the voice, and it was exciting to learn new techniques. I felt as if I was constantly stretching myself. It was difficult stuff, but I just seemed to get it. When you're learning the songs, you're not just learning to sing the notes, but thinking about the underlying emotions and how to feel them in the song. This is what singers called the dynamics. It's not a matter of singing loudly because you can, it's a matter of SINGING LOUDLY BECAUSE YOU'RE PASSIONATE at this point, or singing softly because you're sad.

We kept to a strict timetable, but there was still plenty of time to relax and chat over our meals together. Yvie has a nice husband and two great teenage children who made it very easy for me to fit into the family. In the evenings, Yvie always went to visit her mother, Molly, and one day I asked if I could go with her. I'd spoken to Molly on the phone once or twice during my first lessons with Yvie in London. I liked her sense of humour. She had been a teacher in the village primary school in Methlick, Aberdeenshire, where Yvie grew up. As soon as I met her, I could tell that the children who had been educated by her had been very fortunate. Molly was a vibrant character with such a beaming smile that when you walked into the room you felt as if she were coming over to greet you, even though she couldn't get out of bed.

Although she was paralysed due to an illness, Molly's mind was not affected and she retained her intellect and her sense of humour. When we met, she showed me a poem she liked. I think it illustrates perfectly the special person she was. The title is 'I'm Fine Thank You'.

There is nothing the matter with me,
I'm as healthy as I can be.
I have arthritis in both my knees
And when I talk, I talk with a wheeze,
My pulse is weak and my blood is thin,
But I'm awfully well for the shape I'm in.

Sleep is denied me night after night
But every morning I find I'm all right,
My memory is failing, my head's in a spin
But I'm awfully well for the shape I'm in.

How do I know my youth is all spent?
Well my 'get up and go' has got up and went.
But I really don't mind when I think with a grin,
Of all the grand places my 'get up' has bin.

'Old age is golden', I've heard it said,
But sometimes I wonder as I get into bed,
With my ears in the drawer, my teeth in a cup
My eyes on the table until I wake up.
'Ere sleep overtakes me, I say to myself,
'Is there anything else I could lay on the shelf?'

When I was young, my slippers were red,
I could kick my heels over my head.
When I was older, my slippers were blue,
But still I could dance the whole night through.
Now I am old, my slippers are black,
I walk to the store and puff my way back.

I get up each day and dust off my wits,
And pick up the paper and read the 'obits'.
If my name is still missing, I know I'm not dead,
So I have a good breakfast – and face what's ahead.

An enormous amount of care and thought had gone into choosing what I would sing on my album. Nick Raymonde, who is my A and R guy at Syco, had been through hundreds of possibilities to come up with a very different repertoire from the songs from musicals that I was used to singing, and that, perhaps, people expected from me. Syco's intention was to surprise the world with a unique and interesting combination, and I was very happy with the selection. Some songs were personal favourites of mine, others I liked but might not have thought of singing myself, and a couple were completely new to me, but quickly became favourites.

I'd heard the name Steve Mac many times over recent months. Everybody who spoke about him was unanimous in their opinion: he was a great guy and he would be a fantastic producer for me to work with. So, you can imagine that I was fairly nervous when I first went to the studio to meet him.

The studio itself was situated down a mews street in south-west London. It's a functional-looking building that could easily be the back of any old office in any old town, but when you go inside it's minimalist, modern and full of state-of-the-art equipment.

For someone who has such a great reputation, and has worked with top artists and bands like Leona Lewis and Westlife, Steve Mac was much younger than I was expecting. He has very intense, dark eyes, but a friendly, open smile and the confidence of someone who knows what he's doing. He was a little apprehensive himself because he'd been warned that I could be a wee bit moody, but we clicked straight away.

The studio is a normal-size room with a fairly low ceiling. There are no windows, except the one into Steve's room, where he sits with an engineer who organizes the backing track and records the takes. The studio is air conditioned, so it always feels cool, and there's the facility to change the lighting to suit the mood of the song.

It was all new to me, so I was quite nervous as the door clicked shut behind me and I was all by myself in this dimly lit room standing in front of the mic. I put on the headphones. Steve asked me if I was ready. I gave him the thumbs-up, feeling a wee bit more tentative than I was letting on.

The first track we laid down was 'Cry Me a River'. We decided to try that one first because it was the only song that was going to be on the album that I had recorded before, so I'd probably feel more comfortable with it.

The plangent opening strings transported me immediately into the mood of the song. I closed my eyes.

Now, you say you love me . . .

A lot of water had flowed under the bridge since I first recorded it at Heartbeat Studio on the outskirts of Edinburgh, but, singing in these sophisticated surroundings in the middle of London, I could summon the same emotions: the sadness of love denied, the hollow triumph of revenge.

The notes came as naturally as breathing. Alone with just the music, I felt a rush of satisfaction, as if I had finally found what I'd been looking for all my life.

The studio became my sanctuary. In order to be nearer, I moved out of the convent and into a very nice flat in West London. Each morning, a car would pick me up and take me to the studio and we would work from about eleven until four o'clock in the afternoon. I still longed to go for walks on my own, especially since the new flat I was in was situated near the Royal Botanic Gardens at Kew. I'd like to have seen the colourful flower borders and the exotic tropical plants in the Palm House, but now the recording studio was my escape from the rest of the world.

For me, the studio is like being inside a precious rainbow bubble floating above all the swirling clutter and worry of life. In the studio, it's just me and the music, and I love that pure connection with the song. As soon as I put on the cans, I feel that I have come home to a place where I know I am safe. I become a calm person, a person who knows her value, a person who has been given the great privilege of doing what she does best without any distractions. My only conversation is with the song.

Next, we recorded 'I Dreamed a Dream'. The song had come to symbolize my dream of success, but when I had sung it at my audition I'd been singing about longing to go back to the security of the life I'd enjoyed before losing my mother. Now I was on a new path, and one that I had no doubt that she wanted me to follow, so the song had taken on a subtly different meaning for me.

Steve is a clever guy and knows exactly how to get what he wants from me. Sometimes he'll ask to hear the songs sung in slightly different ways so that he has a range of options when he is mixing the album. I found it really interesting and exciting to stretch to that kind of challenge. I've always enjoyed acting, so when Steve says something like, 'Have a go at singing it as if you were ten years younger,' I relish the opportunity to get into character. I was open to trying anything and Steve found that refreshing. He is a natural enabler – positive and encouraging when you're doing well, but perfectly straightforward when you muck up – and that clarity and honesty meant I trusted him right from the start. When he says, 'That's exactly what I wanted,' I know he's telling the truth, and it gives me a fillip to have pleased him. In turn, I think my growing confidence feeds back to him, creating a special alchemy from our individual talents. It's a great professional chemistry and respect that we have developed. Steve works at a fast pace. It's hard work, but I found I could keep up, and I found the recording process uplifting and exhilarating.

It's a funny feeling singing a hymn with earphones on in a studio instead of openly in church as a member of the congregation, but wherever I am singing I feel closer to God, because He gave me this gift in the first place. I was keen to include the hymn 'How Great Thou Art' because it is the favourite of my friend and teacher Frank Quinn, who has been such a support to me. I think the words of praise sound particularly pure, the message simple and true.

'Amazing Grace' is another very powerful hymn for me because it expresses so beautifully how God is always there, especially when I am scared.

I once was lost but now am found,
Was blind, but now I see.

It is a hymn that was to take on a special meaning for me later on in my journey.

'Who I Was Born to Be' is a song that was written specially for me and the lyrics encapsulate so much about my life. This seems to be the favourite song of many of my fans and whenever I sing it, it feels almost like a rallying cry.

The anger in my voice during the Madonna song 'You'll See' is a strong and productive anger, rather than a frustrated anger that brings bitterness and tears. When I recorded this track, I felt I was singing not only to those bullies at school, but also, to a certain extent, to the media for all the pressure I'd been subjected to. I'm not scared of the media. It's part of the job, part of the territory and I recognize that artists need the press. But I am only human. I'd been built up, then smashed down, but I wasn't going to buckle. When I was singing 'You'll See', I felt I was rebuilding myself, giving myself the push I needed to carry on.

'Up to the Mountain' is a Kelly Clarkson number. This is a song that was chosen for me and I really enjoyed singing it, and 'Daydream Believer' brought back great memories of watching the Monkees on television when I was little. The version on the album is a slow version, so you can really hear the words –

I'd never really noticed them before, but now they had meaning for me. Soon, I hoped, I'd be able to go back to Blackburn. A homecoming queen? We'd have to see about that!

One day when I came into the studio Steve said he had a song he'd like to play to me. It's called 'Proud', and Steve had co-written it. I found it very moving because it's about a conflict between a father and a son.

We've all had conflict with our parents at some stage, and I was no exception. I had a lot of difficulties when I was growing up and, even though I was loved, I always slightly felt as if I was in the way. My parents hadn't intended to have another child at their time of life. I just came along, and then I wasn't an easy child to cope with.

As I grew up, I'd continued to rely on my parents as well as trying to please them. I hadn't given myself much room to be my own person. At the same time, I'd known that if I didn't devote myself to my mum and dad, that would be wrong and I would feel guilty afterwards. So there was a sort of conflict within myself.

The other side of it was that I had always sought my mum's and dad's approval for everything, and now that I didn't have their guidance, life could be very scary.

There's a line in the song that's about being your

own boss, your own individual person. That was something I had been struggling with since my mother died.

For me, the song is also about regret. I'd tried my best, but I didn't honestly feel I'd given my parents anything to be proud of while they were alive. My mother always had faith in my abilities, but she must have been anxious about what I would do after she died. If she could have known what was going to happen, she wouldn't have had all that worry. She would have been so amazed and so proud of me.

The first few times I tried to sing 'Proud', I couldn't do it for crying.

The biggest surprise of the album was probably 'Wild Horses', and that was one of the last songs we recorded. This particular version was picked for me by Simon Cowell and I thought it was a great choice. I knew the song from my youth because my brothers were great Rolling Stones fans, and there was something about the lyrics of the first verse that reminded me of the council estate where I lived and conjured poignant memories of my early upbringing.

When I'm singing the song, I always feel I'm singing from my mother's point of view, as if she's talking to me and I'm the one who's listening, so it is quite an emotional experience.

For the singer I used to be, the inclination would have been to give the first big crescendo a lot of power, but I learned that it is so much more effective if you sing it gently. For that you need a great deal of control so it's technically difficult to achieve, but once you have the control, you can sing quietly, then go loud and come back to quiet again. I think when people first heard me singing 'Wild Horses', they started to take me more seriously as a singer. The record company in the States were certainly very excited about it, and 'Wild Horses' was the song that was chosen for me to sing on my first public performance as a singer in my own right.

34

The Home of the Brave

For most people, a first-class flight and the prospect of five days in a luxury five-star hotel in Los Angeles, with a trip to Disneyland included, would be a once-in-a-lifetime holiday they'd remember all of their lives. But holidays are for relaxation, and I'd already had mine in the wee Scottish resort of Blackburn, West Lothian.

Steve Mac and I worked so well together that the album was made in six weeks, with just a few additional sessions to come later, so I'd been able to have some time off, happily swapping the luxury London flat for my pebble-dash council house, my entourage of assistants and bodyguards for neighbours, family and friends. I'd been able to go to Mass in Our Lady of Lourdes and visit the Whitburn Legion of Mary. I'd dined out on my favourite holiday supper of fish and chips.

In Blackburn, with familiar people and things around me, I knew who I was and what I was doing.

During this whole process, I've never for one minute wished I could return to how things were before, but I've never seen why I should become a different person in order to pursue the path that I'm on. The way I see it is that I am the same person, but I am growing, exploring a potential that has always been there but that I wasn't able to fulfil at an earlier stage in my life. I'm fully aware that I am very lucky to have this opportunity, and I'm very grateful for all the gifts and luxuries that seem to accompany fame, but I just don't care very much about material things. As long as I have clothes I can wear, food to eat and I can sing, I'm quite happy. My parents worked hard so that us kids didn't want for anything, but they also taught us that the greatest gifts are not in this world.

'Can we open the window?' I asked, as the plane bound for Los Angeles began to taxi towards the runway.

Ciaran, my bodyguard, looked at me in alarm, but when he saw my face he realized I was joking. People never know quite what to expect with me.

Laughing was the only way I could disguise the sheer and utter panic that was throbbing through my whole body. We were in first class on a British Airways flight. The space and service in the upstairs lounge takes away some of the strain of flying, but nothing could alter the fact that we were about to spend nine hours in the air, the longest I'd ever flown, and I was terrified.

The purpose of the trip was my first appearance as a professional singer in my own right, and all sorts of questions were looming that could not be answered until the moment I stood up and sang in front of the audience on the biggest television programme in America, the final of *America's Got Talent*. The main question was, could I do it?

There were two days before that, I kept telling myself, so there wasn't any point in panicking yet. I might as well enjoy myself until then. When that tactic didn't work, I tried to think about all the times that I'd got up in front of an audience and managed to deliver a song against the odds. Thoughts like that should help, but they don't, because nerves aren't rational. You can be as logical as you like, but it doesn't stop your heart racing and your brain overloading. The logic should be that the more performances you give, the less nervous you become, but it doesn't seem to work like that. I know that I'm not unique in this because people keep telling me that lots of performers with years of experience still get paralysed by stage fright. It doesn't really help when everyone around you is saying it's going to be fine. They're not the ones who have to get up there! Anyway, on this occasion I knew that, whatever they said, they were really thinking that it was a very big deal indeed.

One of the great pleasures of my new life is the fact that I seem to make people happy. I haven't worked out quite why this is, but it's a very nice and surprising feeling, so I've decided that it's probably best not to over-analyse, but just enjoy. When we disembarked at Los Angeles airport, there must have been two thousand fans waiting to greet me. When I was a kid, I used to watch newsreel of the Beatles arriving at airports. There were crowds of fans, screaming and stretching out their hands to try to touch them, and I can remember wondering at the time, how did all those people know the Beatles were arriving then? How come their parents allowed them to go to the airport? My fans are generally a wee bit older than those teenage girls, but I still didn't understand how they knew when I was arriving, or how they'd managed to take time off work to come to see me. It took us ages to get to the car, and then we had a police escort to the hotel. I felt more like a visiting head of state than a singer. I do appreciate all the effort people made to welcome me, but it was also rather bewildering.

I was staying at the Hotel Bel-Air, one of the most iconic hotels in the world. I was there just before it closed for a major refurbishment, but I cannot really imagine how they're going to make it any better because it was absolutely beautiful, with all the little Spanish-style houses, painted pink with red tiles on the roof, amid luscious gardens and pools. It was a blisteringly hot, sunny day and the cool blue oval pool looked very inviting, even to someone who has never learned to swim. As I walked past the sun-loungers to my suite, it was almost like having déjà vu, because I'd seen the setting so many times in films. I kept expecting one of the slim, tanned women on the sun-loungers to take off her sunglasses and reveal herself as the young Elizabeth Taylor, or for Cary Grant to put down his newspaper and wink at me. My name would now join a list of guests that included Grace Kelly and Marilyn Monroe. I hope it doesn't sound ungrateful when I say that that knowledge didn't make it any easier to relax in my plushly furnished living room.

Disneyland is a place I'd always wanted to visit and it was as magical as I'd expected it to be, but really to enjoy a place like that you need to be with family, or friends you know well, so you can let yourself go back to childhood glee and excitement. It's just not the same flying up in the air on a pastel elephant accompanied by professional colleagues and a body-guard. You're aware that every yelp and silly face you make is being photographed, so even though the visit was arranged to take my mind off things, I couldn't really relax. Inevitably that led to some clever head-lines back home about Glumbo on Dumbo!

The dress I was wearing for *America's Got Talent* was designed by Suzanne Neville. I'd been to the final fitting in London a couple of days before our trip to

Los Angeles. It was a plain, full-length black satin evening gown with just a few crystals to catch the light, but it was cut beautifully to give me the best possible shape. When I travel, the dress I'm wearing has to travel with me. It doesn't quite get its own seat, but we don't put it in cargo just in case it doesn't come out at the other end. On this occasion, my manager Andy carried it on board.

'That'll look smashing on you!' I joked as we were getting on to the plane.

Andy's OK. It would take a lot more than that to get him embarrassed. That first trip to the States was where I really got to know him, because when you're travelling you spend so much time together. On a long flight you see each other bored, you see each other tired, you hear each other snoring. There's nowhere to hide. Andy's a great one for banter, and we can amuse ourselves for hours playing 'Name That Tune', or 'Name the Artist'. All those years of listening to the radio have given me a practically encyclopaedic knowledge of pop from the sixties, seventies and eighties, but Andy gives me a run for my money because he's been in the music business since the sixties himself.

Andy's presence is very reassuring. He's managed acts as famous as George Michael and Geri Halliwell, so he's seen it all before and there's nobody he doesn't know. When we arrived at the studios for *America's Got Talent* I knew that at least one of us knew what he was doing.

You'd think putting on that dress would be the easy bit. Was it heck! With a tight-fitting garment like that, it's like trying to get a cork back into a champagne bottle, so you have to wear your Spanx underneath to smooth you out. I never knew my body had so much flesh. I'm not kidding. Those Spanx are murder to get on. You need two people pulling them up, so that's professional distance gone for a start, then you have to try to do the dress up, and that required a foot on my backside to hold it all together in order to get the zip up. As far as adopting a sophisticated persona was concerned, it felt more like I was in a pantomime of Cinderella. I didn't know whether I'd be able to breathe, let alone sing, and when I tried to walk I felt like a penguin with constipation. That's what it takes to look elegant. At least it was a distraction!

The great thing about making my debut on *America's Got Talent* was that, although I was in a foreign country, I was surrounded by people I knew. Yvie is the voice coach on the show, so she was there already, and we were able to do a warm-up together before the rehearsals. On the day, with the audience in, there was also Piers Morgan, who is one of the three judges on the programme.

I was extremely nervous about going on stage. Piers and Sharon Osborne came backstage to see me and were very encouraging. Everyone was reassuring me that it wouldn't matter if I mucked up because it was only a pre-record. I would be singing in front of an audience of hundreds, but if I made a mistake then it wouldn't go out to an audience of millions. To me, that sounded like it was going to be a disaster, if not a catastrophe. It took me quite a while to pluck up the courage to go on, but eventually I was brave enough to step up. As soon as the music starts, it's like a switch with me. I start singing, and all the other stuff goes away.

We did two takes, then someone took a DVD up to Simon Cowell's house to see which one he wanted to have shown. It was as simple as that! Suddenly, all the worry had gone because I'd done it! I'd sung a song nobody had heard me sing before. Now, the largest television audience of the year in America would see me singing 'Wild Horses' for the first time. Only then did it dawn on me what a debut this was. It felt pretty good. In fact, it felt so good I wanted to do it again!

The second time I went to the States I was no less nervous, but things were a lot easier, because in the meantime I'd been lucky enough to persuade my niece Joanne to come and work as my personal assistant. Joanne lives in Bathgate, just down the road from Blackburn, and she'd been very supportive to me after my mother died as well as during the time when I was holed up in Yule Terrace surrounded by the press. Joanne's an efficient, no-nonsense sort of person, with a great sense of humour like her mother, Bridie. Because I've known her since she was born, there's no barrier when it comes to personal moments like getting my dress on, and because she's family I trust her implicitly and don't have to watch what I say all the time. Joanne's very stylish herself, so she helps me pick out suitable casual clothes to wear when I'm not on stage. There's only one problem: I have asked her to stop calling me Auntie Susan, because I don't think it sounds very professional.

On the second trip to Los Angeles, we were staying in the Peninsula Hotel. My day of 'relaxation' on this occasion was a tour of Universal Studios, which I really enjoyed because Joanne and Andy came along too. We toured round the sets of several films I had seen, such as *War of the Worlds* and *The Da Vinci Code*, as well as *Jaws*. That was a laugh, because as we passed the pool where some of the action shots were staged, this huge shark suddenly reared up out of the water, soaking us all. I screamed and jumped so high I almost landed in Andy's lap!

When we arrived at the studios for *Dancing with the Stars*, there was another slightly surreal experience as the lift doors opened and standing there was the head judge, Len Goodman, whom I'd seen so many times on *Strictly Come Dancing*, the British version of the show.

'Oh hello!' I greeted him as if he were an old friend.

It's funny when you see famous people, because sometimes you feel you know them so well you forget you've never actually met them. It turned out that Len was a fan of mine too and liked my singing.

On the programme I sang 'I Dreamed a Dream', which was slightly less stressful than singing 'Wild Horses' because it's a song I've sung quite a lot in public now. The only complication was when this dancing couple appeared writhing in front of me, doing a very dangerous-looking routine involving some impossible lifts. I knew that if I looked at them I'd be tempted to say, 'Don't drop her, for God's sake!' It took an extra bit of concentration to focus on my own performance.

To be honest, the first part of that trip is a bit of a blur now, because of what happened next.

It wasn't a total surprise, because I was told in advance that he would be paying me a visit, but I couldn't believe it until I opened the door of my suite and saw Donny Osmond standing there with a big bunch of flowers for me. Actually, I still didn't believe it then. Oh my God! Donny Osmond was giving me a kiss on the cheek! I touched my face to check that it was real.

Thirty-five years after I first fell for him, Donny is just as handsome, with those big smashing eyes and that sparkling smile, and he has a really good sense of humour to go with it. He needed it, I can tell you, because I was so flustered and excited I wasn't making any sense at all at the beginning. At first, I could do nothing but giggle. I was actually trying discreetly to pinch myself to see if I was awake.

Donny was everything I wanted him to be. Very good looking, very charming, but a normal kind of guy. When I'd calmed down, we were able to talk a little about how you deal with fame. For both of us it's very important to have close contact with our families, and he understood my need to feel grounded, which is why I am at home in Scotland. He could relate to that.

Some of our encounter was being filmed for a television special about me that was going to be shown at Christmas. People have asked me what the heck Donny and I were laughing at so much, so I'll tell you.

We sat down together on the sofa and one of the crew gave me a mic to position on my chest. My hand was shaking so much, it got stuck in the zip.

'Would you like a hand with that?' Donny asked, with a twinkle in his beautiful eyes.

'You're not going down my blouse!' I responded, quick as a flash.

All those nights I'd stared at the picture of Donny Osmond on my wall at home! I'd never have believed that I'd one day be sitting on a sofa joking with him.

We just doubled up.

When I look back over this amazing year I've had, meeting Donny Osmond has to be the personal high point for me and it's a memory that I will treasure for ever.

*   *   *

My next trip to America was for yet another 'most important performance' of my life. As soon as you've accomplished one thing, there's always another marker to hit. I think maybe that's why I can never quite trust the success I've had. Maybe one day there'll come a time when I'll know what I'm doing and it will hold no fear for me, but that hasn't happened yet because the pressure's ratcheted up with each challenge. It doesn't get much bigger than launching your debut album live on coast-to-coast American television. Does it?

November had already been a very hectic month. I'd been to Los Angeles, met Donny Osmond, had only two days back in Scotland to wallow in the afterglow of that experience, before travelling to London again and then on Eurostar to Paris to sing on a television programme there. On that occasion, I managed to put my heel through my dress as I stepped out on stage, and heard a worrying rip, but I kept on going, because that's what you do. Back in London, I'd had dress fittings, and voice coaching with Yvie, who was back in London herself because the *The X Factor* was on television. I then recorded a performance of 'Wild Horses' for the *The X Factor*, before flying the next day to New York. The following morning I was due to perform live on the *Today Show*, singing three songs in the open air of Rockefeller Plaza.

Usually, in the build-up to a performance, I might get that funny butterfly feeling in my stomach a couple of weeks before and say to myself, 'Come on now, Susan! It's not for a while yet.' And as long as I've got something else to think about, then I can keep the wobbles at bay. But the nearer the event, the worse it gets, and even though I try to kid myself and the people around me that I'm fine by making jokes and laughing a lot, the nerves are building up inside me like steam in a pressure cooker. The weird thing is that as the time runs down to the performance, it doesn't feel like nerves any more. A kind of dread overwhelms my whole personality, as if all the in-securities I've ever had in my life and all the unsolved problems that I've still got to deal with are swallow-ing me up. I don't know why this happens, but I'm hoping that it's something I can learn to control, because it's not a nice feeling for me or for anyone around me.

In New York, I'd barely had a chance to feel the usual build-up, because I'd been so busy and I was already tired before I started, so it all seemed to come at once, whoosh, like a mud slide engulfing me. I didn't sleep a wink in the hotel the night before. All night, the wall of fear towered mountainously above me and by the morning I had convinced myself that I would never climb it. Unable to face the world, I decided to hide. When Joanne came to give me my wake-up call at five o'clock, the door was locked and

I wouldn't let her in. Alarmed, Joanne called Andy, but even his calm, reassuring voice through the door wouldn't make me open it. Andy is a resourceful chap, so he managed to get a pass key from one of the chambermaids. He found me still in the shirt and jeans I had been wearing when he said goodnight the evening before, my face all red from crying.

Andy is very gentle and calm, but time was ticking on, so he had to set out the choice for me. At 8.30 I was due to go live across America. It was now approaching seven.

'No one is putting a gun to your head, Susan. You can do whatever you want. But all your life you've waited for this moment, and it's up to you. We can walk. We can go back to the airport now and fly straight home and forget all about this, or we can go out there and show them what you're made of.'

The real decider was when he added, 'Just so you know, there's lots of ladies who have flown from all over the States to be there and support you today. They've been there since half past four in the morning, and what a shame to let them down as well . . .'

I didn't want to let all those ladies down, nor Andy, nor any of the people around me who had put in a lot of effort to try to help me. This was the launch of my album and they were depending on me. If I didn't do my bit, it would all fall apart.

That's when I thought of another voice – my mother's. She would have put it a different way:

'Now look, Susan, stop giving these guys a hard time. So come on, pull yourself together, or I'll skelp your arse!'

I went out into that ice-cold New York morning shivering with fear. It felt very strange to be outside in the grey light of early morning when I was used to studios and artificial lights. Surrounded by Manhattan skyscrapers, standing in Rockefeller Plaza feels like being at the bottom of a well, almost too scary to look up. It's a setting I'd seen often in the movies, but I'd never imagined I'd ever be there myself. The air was so chilly that my breath puffed out frosty clouds. In front of me were hundreds of people cheering and waving red scarves. Never in my life had I felt so exposed. It was all I could do to stop myself rushing off stage to hide again. But when the musical director pressed play, I magically switched from a terrified wee lassie to Susan Boyle, performer. People who have seen the way I am backstage say that it is astonishing to witness the transformation. Suddenly, the love coming from that crowd warmed me right through to my bones. I was doing what I was born to do.

Afterwards, a group of my fans presented me with a quilt they had made specially for me. Bordered with fifty-two mostly red squares, all embroidered with moving and supportive messages, there are forty-nine original appliquéd designs sewn on to squares of blue, green, white and red fabric, each one decorated

345

with a thoughtful message from individual quilters all over the world. Each image is different, from an angel to a penguin. There are too many to describe here, but every one is unique and represents something significant about my life. On the central square is a simple message embroidered on a white background: 'Susan, We love you.'

I'd never had anything created for me before, let alone a beautiful object like this, which really is a work of art. So much imagination and effort had gone into that quilt, so much kindness and care, it was like a symbol of the faith people had in me. I knew I didn't deserve anything so marvellous, and it was all I could do to keep control of my emotions, but when the quilters presented me with a wee miniature quilt for Pebbles too, my overwhelming gratitude swelled up inside me and flooded out in unstoppable tears. This time, they were tears of joy.

35

Europe

One of the things I had no knowledge of before becoming a professional singer was the sheer number of people who have to be involved to create one moment on stage or on television. As part of the promotion for the album, I have been asked to appear on shows all over Europe. I have travelled to France, Germany, Italy, Denmark, Spain and Holland. Each time, a phenomenal amount of organization goes into making the two minutes I'm on stage happen.

Andy and Joanne always travel with me. There are also usually at least a couple of people from Sony and Syco, like Melissa and Alex, who have one eye on what's going on and the other firmly glued to their Blackberry. Sometimes I have a bodyguard, and there are always several technical people, like Jonathan, the sound guy, who gets to the venue before me and sets up the musical side correctly. Sometimes there's a producer as well, and that's just the personnel on the record company side. In addition, there are all the staff from the television studio to meet and greet and fuss around me. Sometimes the head of Sony in the country we're visiting will put in an appearance. It can get a wee bit overwhelming, and generally I like to be in the dressing room with just Joanne and Michelle, my hair and make-up lady.

I first met Michelle when she came up to Scotland when we were filming the television special at a hotel on Loch Lomond. She'd had quite a journey to get there. Michelle always travels with a suitcase full of make-up and hairdressing equipment. On the Heathrow Express, she had been texting and hadn't noticed when an old lady mistook her case for her own and got off at Terminal 3 with it. So when Michelle came to get off at Terminal 5, there was only a case with a Thai airlines sticker on it. Trying to think logically, she rushed back to Terminal 3, to the Thai Airlines desk, but they couldn't help her, except to suggest she report the incident to the police, which she did, but now time was running out for her flight. It was the first time she'd worked with me and she desperately didn't want to turn up late, so Michelle took the decision to go back to Terminal 5 without the case and buy as many of the things she needed as she could in duty-free. But just as she arrived there, her phone rang and it was the police saying they'd got her bag at Terminal 3, so she decided to race back again. She only just caught her flight.

I only heard this story much later, after Michelle

had accompanied me on several trips, and I'd never have guessed what she'd just been through when I first met her, because then, and ever since, she has always appeared fresh as a daisy and totally un-flappable. Michelle says it's amazing what you can do with a bit of make-up!

You need nice people around you, because there is so much waiting around in dressing rooms that you'd start climbing the walls if you didn't have friends to keep you calm. I find the process of having my hair washed and styled and my make-up put on very relaxing. We go for as natural a look as possible, a kind of polished version of me. The only bit I can't get used to is the acrylic nails. Michelle and I call them Britain's Got Talons. I'm always nervously trying to pick them off even before I get to the stage.

Half an hour before my call, we start to get me into the dress I'm wearing, but first of all it's squeezing into my wee Spanx with Joanne at the front and Michelle at the back struggling to pull them up and all three of us trying not to topple over laughing. Then it's into one of three dresses. They're all by Suzanne Neville. There's a beautiful burgundy silk one with tiers all the way down, a midnight-blue one that is diamante from top to bottom, and the black satin one with diamante that I wore for *America's Got Talent*. We have to remember to put on my jewellery, and it's round about this time that I have my warm-up with Yvie.

When I'm travelling round Europe, it would be impossible for Yvie to accompany me everywhere, but we do always manage to get a warm-up by telephone. From my end in the dressing room, that's quite straightforward. We do the Vvvvvvvs, and all the other breathing exercises, with her singing them and me singing them back. I'm often trying to put my shoes on at the same time, or Joanne's trying to fasten a necklace for me, but at least I'm in one place. Down the line for Yvie, it's not quite so simple. Because Europe is an hour ahead, very often when I'm about to go on stage, Yvie's on her way home from work. She'll frequently find herself at the station trying to hide behind a coffee kiosk, with all the train announcements going on in the background. Sometimes she is actually on the train in between the carriages, singing the exercises to me, and when she goes to sit down after we've finished all the other commuters look at her a wee bit strangely. Yvie has warmed me up in shop doorways, on garage forecourts, through a speaker phone in her car, and at the nursing home when she's been visiting Molly. A lot of the ladies there really enjoyed it!

One of the unexpected pleasures about travelling and performing is all the people you bump into. Being famous yourself is like a passport to speaking to people you'd never have dared talk to before, like Anne Robinson, whom I met in the first-class lounge at Heathrow airport. In real life she's a very nice person, not at all strict like she is on *The Weakest Link*. La Toya Jackson was appearing on the same show as me during one of my trips to Germany. Then when I was in Amsterdam in March, there was a knock on my dressing-room door and who should poke his familiar tattooed torso round the door but Demi, the father in Stavros Flatley. We had a great old chat about what we'd been doing since the tour. He and his son Lagi had been all over the world and written a book themselves.

One of the drawbacks of celebrity is that I don't really get a chance to appreciate all the wonderful places I'm visiting. The best way to see a city is by wandering around on your own, taking in all the sights, sounds and smells, and watching the little everyday dramas unfolding in shops, cafés and parks. The trouble with my face being so recognizable now is that I *am* the drama. I'm no longer somebody on the outside looking in; I'm the centre of attention. Sometimes I wish that I had an invisibility cloak like Harry Potter so I could wander around unnoticed again.

Often, if I have a few hours' waiting before a performance, the thing I most want to do is go for a walk to relieve some of the tension building up in my body, but wherever I go my face is recognized and I can't make much progress, because I'm constantly being stopped for photographs. The only alternative is to sit in a hotel room looking out of the window. I'm always lucky enough to stay in gorgeous hotels, with fantastic views, but sometimes it can feel as if I'm vacuum-packed in a sterile environment.

There was one wonderful exception to this, arranged by my friend Frank on one of my trips to Paris. A car drove me and Andy to the rue du Bac, where the headquarters of the Daughters of Charity of St Vincent de Paul are situated. Although there were paparazzi following the car and all the motor-drives were going off as I stepped out on the street, they weren't allowed into the convent. Sister Loreto, a lovely Irish nun, took us inside, shielding me from the attention, and for a moment, with all the paparazzi poking their cameras through the iron gates, I was reminded of the family in *The Sound of Music* finding shelter from the chase.

The convent is built of the pale gold stone typical of the elegant older buildings of Paris and it is set round a peaceful courtyard. Sister Loreto explained the history of the order, which was founded in 1633 for the purpose of serving the needs of the poor and sick, by St Vincent de Paul, a French priest, and St Louise de Marillac, who was a widow. I had always been aware of the work that the St Vincent de Paul Society did with people of disability in Scotland. As I mentioned earlier, St Joseph's residential home in Rosewell was the place that Pope John Paul II visited on his pastoral trip to our country in 1982 and it was there that Frank Quinn met him. Now the society's work is carried on mainly in the community, but the convent in rue du Bac is the mother house of the organization. The sisters, who wear a blueish-grey habit, live in a community there in order to develop the spiritual life.

Sister Loreto and I went into the chapel and prayed together. Kneeling in the cool silence, I was able to reconnect with everything that is really important and to find serenity in the heart of a bustling city.

36

Television Special

For someone who has watched television all her life, and was, in a sense, created by television, the idea that there was going to be a Christmas television special devoted to my story was yet another unbelievable step on my weird and wonderful journey. I was thrilled when they told me that Piers Morgan was going to present the studio part of the programme, because I've always liked Piers but, more than that, I feel that he's always given me all the support he can. When times have been tough, Piers has gone out there and stuck up for me, and he was there at the very start, so I couldn't think of a better person to host the show.

The great thing about Piers is that you can have a laugh with him, and there were some honeys of outtakes on that programme, like the moment when a member of the audience shouted out, 'Can you do the wiggle?'

I turned to Piers and said, 'Can you do the wiggle?'

Well, Piers may be a lot of things, but he did a pretty feeble wiggle, I have to tell you. So I decided to show him how!

Later on, when they had the smoke machine going for one of my songs, there were clouds of the stuff wafting around the stage. I looked at Piers, and asked, 'My God, what was that?'

'What?' he said.

'Did you fart?'

'No!' he said.

'Well someone did – look at the mess it's made!'

Note to self: Try to resist the jokes and be more of a lady, Susan!

The audience seemed to like it, anyway. They were all doubled up laughing.

If the 'Donny moment' was a personal favourite on my journey, then the 'Elaine Paige moment' was the musical high point. We sang 'I Know Him So Well' from *Chess*, the song with which Elaine Paige and Barbara Dixon had a number-one hit in 1985. I clearly remembered them singing in the video on *Top of the Pops*, both of them with big eighties hair, and Elaine Paige in a white silk shirt and black leggings on a kind of studio chessboard. Years ago I had sung the Elaine Paige part myself at a karaoke night at The Turf in Blackburn, but this was some contrast.

Here was a woman whose voice I had admired for so many years. It had been my dream to be like her, and now I was singing with her. The atmosphere in the studio was absolutely electric and I was so excited we had to do a few takes to get it right, but it really was an indescribable feeling of delight to be singing a duet with my heroine. I am so grateful to have had that opportunity. It was one of those moments that will go into my jukebox of memories and always remain there whatever the future holds.

In the middle of the show, there was a wonderful surprise when Piers presented me with my triple platinum album. At the time of writing, I have sold nine million copies of the CD worldwide and people tell me that it's some sort of record. Sometimes I try to picture all those copies in all those living rooms all over the country, but it's just too many to think about. What I do know for sure is that I have made an album that people of all nationalities and faiths like to listen to. That is an achievement beyond my wildest dreams and something of which I'm very proud.

I've spent my whole life trying to prove to people that I could do something. It was a promise I made to my mother, but it was also a promise I made to myself. I dedicated the album, as I dedicate this book, to my beloved mother. I know that she would be proud of me. I also know that she would think it was all really funny. She would have killed herself laughing at some of the things that have happened. Even though she didn't have an easy life, my mother could laugh about anything. There was nothing she loved more.

37

Celebrity

I've come to realize over the past year that the nature of celebrity is paradoxical. It bring pleasures as well as pressures. It brings freedom, but also restriction. Sometimes one side seems to outweigh the other and the trick is to try to keep everything in balance. I'm learning all the time.

Because I'm travelling so much, Pebbles now stays in London with a very nice lady. I miss her company, but she's a wee bit old now to make the trip back up.

I can be myself in Blackburn. When I go shopping at Tesco, people say hello, but they give me space. We've all got our lives to get on with. Modern technology such as mobile phones, YouTube and Twitter, which were responsible for catapulting me to fame a year ago, now make it difficult for me to go much further afield on my own.

In January I decided to break with routine and be normal for a wee while, so I took a bus to Bathgate Station and then the train into Edinburgh. It was kind of quiet at Bathgate Station, so I thought I would be OK. When I got on the train, there were a couple of people in the carriage with me who said hello. They must have texted their friends, because by the next stop it was ten, the next, twenty, and by the time I arrived in Edinburgh there was a whole platform of people waiting for me. I felt like the Pied Piper with this crowd trailing around after me. I went into a department store to get out of the way, but they all followed me in. I asked to see the manager for help, but he wanted to get his picture taken with me as well! Was I safe on the bus to Musselburgh, where my brother Gerard lives? Was I heck! It was like being on a bus with an enormous Christmas tree. I was causing havoc.

When Andy read about my excursion in the paper the next day, he said, 'You went on a bus? You could have hopped in a taxi!'

'It would have cost me fifty quid to get a taxi!' I told him.

It's not just about the money. I like being outside in the air. I prefer a train journey to a journey by car. I like being normal. It's what I'm used to. But it's getting increasingly difficult and I'm reluctantly having to accept that it's no longer practical for me to do things just like everybody else.

The other side of it is that there are fantastic opportunities open to me that I wouldn't have without my fame. Andy got me tickets for the Spandau

Ballet reunion tour concert in Glasgow. I took some friends with me and the doorman at the SECC recognized me from when I came to do my original audition, so they escorted us in and we all got five-star treatment. Afterwards we went backstage and I met Tony Hadley and the Kemp brothers, who are even better looking in real life. When I meet people who have been heroes of mine, I'm still a wee fan myself. I think that's why I'm always ready to sign autographs or have my photo taken. On the way back home, my friends and I were hungry so we stopped at the Kentucky Fried Chicken. There were two old ladies who'd been to the pictures having a bite to eat as well. They asked if they could phone someone and tell them who they were there with. Of course I didn't mind. It goes with the territory.

Another hilarious thing happened just after Christmas when Lorraine's daughter took her kids to see a pantomime at the King's Theatre in Edinburgh. A well-known Scottish television star called Allan Stewart was starring in it and apparently he did an impersonation of me in the middle of the show. When they reported this back to me, I couldn't wait to get tickets myself, especially as I've been an admirer of Allan Stewart's for years.

We arrived at the final performance and the management met me and asked if I'd like to go on stage myself to surprise him. Well, as you may have gathered, there's a bit of a devil in me, so I said,

'Right, let's do it!' They said that they would come down and get me at 5.30. I watched the first part of the pantomime and it was very funny. Then, as arranged, I went backstage.

I couldn't help thinking, as I stood there in the wings, of all the plays I'd come to see in this theatre and all the effort I'd put into my acting classes to train myself to go on stage. Now it was quite peculiar to watch one of Scotland's best-known actors walking down the stage acting out the part of me. He was singing 'I Dreamed a Dream of Wild Horses' dressed in a wig and a gold dress just like mine. I wouldn't have minded, but he had the better-looking legs!

I waited until the song came to the end and he was doing all his patter, then I walked on with a great big scowl on my face, as if I was very angry, and marched right up to him. I stood there for a wee second eyeballing him, then I gave him a big cuddle. It brought the house down!

I said, 'You look better in that frock than I ever have, but you cannae do the wiggle, can ye?'

He said, 'I can!'

And he tried it, but I said, 'Naah! That's not the wiggle. This is how you do it, OK?'

And then I went off again.

It was a bit of a risk, because I didn't know how Allan Stewart would take it, but he was really good about it. It was such a laugh.

I had a couple of weeks off over Christmas, so

Bridie invited me over on Christmas Day. It was the same crowd, except for my brother Joe, as the previous Christmas. Since then my circumstances had changed beyond recognition, but my siblings didn't treat me any differently. We ate our turkey dinner and drank a wee glass of wine just like any other family in the land and I have to say, it was bloody fantastic!

The end of the year is always a time of reflection, when you review what's happened and look forward to what's to come. Christmas 2009 felt particularly Christmassy because there was so much snow around. During the first week of January, I was invited to a New Year party at the Cardinal's house in Edinburgh. There had been another fall of snow just before we arrived in the walled front garden. The lights from the house shone a warm, magical glow over the pristine white surfaces and there was that hush that sometimes follows just after the snow has stopped. My footsteps crumped across the frozen whiteness to the statue of Our Lady, where I said a prayer.

The warm, convivial atmosphere inside was such a contrast to the icy tranquillity outside, I could feel my cheeks turning pink. I recognized all sorts of distinguished people there, including the then Secretary of State for Scotland Jim Murphy, the Attorney General, the head of the Church of Scotland, and Sister Patricia Fallon from the Daughters of Charity, who had recently celebrated the seventieth anniversary of her profession. If I hadn't been with my friends Frank, Maureen, Mario and Lorraine, I might have felt a wee bit out of my depth. However, I found a comfortable armchair in the Cardinal's living room and there was no need to worry about not knowing the other guests, because people kept coming up to shake my hand and congratulate me. Most amazing of all was when I glanced at the Cardinal's mantelpiece and saw, propped up amongst all his personal photographs, a copy of my album, with my own photograph smiling out of it.

I've been lucky enough to have been given several awards, such as Great Scot Award 2009 and Glenfiddich Spirit of Scotland Award 2009.

My name is suddenly on the invitation list for parties that previously I would only have read about in *Hello!* magazine. In March, I spent an especially memorable and enjoyable evening at the Thistle Hotel in Glasgow at a tribute to Tommy Gemmell, the legendary footballer who scored the equalizer for Celtic before the Lisbon Lions went on to win the European Cup in 1967. That was the occasion when I wished I had my father with me. I know Dad would have been delighted that I'd met the Cardinal; he would have been astonished that I'd had a number-one album; but getting to shake the hand of Tommy Gemmell, now that was really something!

I hope I'll never lose sight of how privileged I am to have all these opportunities, but the events that I enjoy most are those where I feel that I am using my celebrity to make a difference to other people. Just before Christmas, I visited a Catholic primary school where Mario's daughter Lisa Maria is headteacher. Originally I was scheduled to see the Christmas nativity play in the local church hall, but because of the weather they'd had to cancel the performance, so the children were all disappointed. None of them had been told that I would be visiting, so when I arrived they went wild. I was immediately pulled into their games and their dancing. I think it was the most fun I've ever had at school! But there was one boy I noticed sitting sadly in the corner, so I asked Lisa Maria if there was something the matter with the wee fella. She told me that he had lost his father just a couple of months before and he was pining for him. My heart went out to the lad. I knew just how he was feeling. So I went and sat beside him and I found myself telling him, 'I came here today to see all the children. But I came especially for you!'

His face lit up. I'd given him something different to think about, if only for a few minutes. It's moments like that that make you think that you're doing something worthwhile.

38

Amazing Grace

When you get to my age, you're generally not too bothered whether people remember your birthday. In some ways you'd rather they didn't! So I was surprised when Andy called to ask whether I'd like to spend the day in Japan.

I'd already been to Tokyo to appear on a New Year show and I had recorded an extra track for the Japanese edition of my album, called 'Wings to Fly'. Since its release, the album had gone platinum in Japan and the people from Sony were keen for me to go over again. I assumed they were talking about another promotional opportunity, where I would sing one of my songs for a television programme.

'No, it's something a bit different.'

Andy explained that 1 April is a very important day in the Japanese calendar. It's the beginning of their financial year and it's also the day that students graduate from college. The song 'Wings to Fly' was of particular significance because it is traditionally sung to students on that day.

'They'd like me to sing it at a graduation ceremony?' I guessed.

'Not exactly,' said Andy. 'They were thinking of an eighty-piece orchestra at the Budokan. Do you know what the Budokan is?'

I hadn't got past 'eighty-piece orchestra'.

'It's the venue where the Beatles played,' Andy continued. 'Seats about nine thousand—'

'You are kidding?' I interrupted.

'I'm not kidding—'

'Do you think I'm ready for that?' I eventually whispered down the phone.

'Of course I do,' he said. 'But it doesn't matter what I or anyone else thinks. It's how *you* feel about it. Nobody's going to have a problem if you say no. But if you're up for it, then I think you'll have a great time . . .'

Oh my God! I had never sung in front of a live orchestra before. When I put down the phone I did one of my little jigs on the spot. The idea was great, but my tummy was already bubbling with that strange, almost chemical, reaction you get when you combine excitement with nerves. You're fizzing so much you think you might take off and fly, but at the same time you're frozen to the spot with terror.

Over the next few days I tried to think it through rationally. This was just another step, wasn't it?

Wasn't this what being a professional was all about? Wasn't this the life I had claimed to want? When Yvie Burnett agreed to come along to support me, I began to believe that I could do it. In fact, I was really starting to look forward to it. Joanne and I made plans to go out shopping to buy some clothes for the trip.

A week before we were due to fly, Yvie called me. I could tell straight away from the timbre of her voice that something was wrong. She told me her beloved mother, Molly, had died.

Memories of Molly's courage and fantastic sense of humour in the face of her illness flooded through my mind, washing away all other thoughts. I was so sad, not just for Molly, but because of the hollowness in Yvie's normally bright, businesslike voice. I recognized that and I wanted to be able to support her, but I knew that losing your mother can be very lonely and there's nothing anyone else can do to make you feel better.

'There *is* something you can do,' Yvie told me. Then she asked me to sing at Molly's funeral.

Yvie knows many singers, but I think she asked me because she knew that I understood what it was to be close to your mother and to feel as devastated as she was feeling.

Joanne and I went shopping, as planned, but what we bought was a black suit for me to wear at the funeral. On the Saturday, a car drove us on the long journey north to Aberdeenshire. It had been a hard winter and there were dirty mounds of frozen slush by the side of the country roads. The trees were still holding their leaves in tight buds to protect against the frost. Under a cold grey sky, it almost felt as if the Scottish countryside was in mourning.

On each seat in the wee stone church in the village of Methlick there was an Order of Service with Molly's vibrant face smiling from it. Printed on the back was that poem she loved so much, 'I'm Fine Thank You'. It was so tragic to know that we wouldn't see that smile again, nor hear her laughter.

The congregation sang Psalm 23, 'The Lord Is My Shepherd'. The vicar spoke, but I hardly heard what he was saying because it was my turn next.

I told myself I must not crumble. This time, I was the one who had to be strong. I remembered all the times we had practised the song, but I was shaking as I rose to my feet.

Singing a first note a cappella is like making a leap of faith, but with the help of God, I sang

> *Amazing Grace, how sweet the sound*
> *That saved a wretch like me.*
> *I once was lost but now am found*
> *Was blind, but now I see.*

and my voice became stronger with every word.

After the funeral, we weren't able to stay too long because it was a long journey home. As I hugged her goodbye, I promised Yvie that if she ever wanted to talk, at any time of night or day, I'd be there at the end of the phone. I wanted her to know that she had the support of someone who had experienced what she was going through.

'I know,' she said, squeezing my hand. 'Thank you. But I'll see you on Monday.'

Surely she didn't mean she was still coming to Japan?

'It's my job,' Yvie reassured me. 'It might even help me if I have to focus on something else . . .'

I know how professional Yvie is, and I was so moved I started crying all over again.

Having hugged each other tight in a peaceful little country churchyard, thirty-six hours later we found ourselves hugging again in the buzzing luxury of the Virgin Upper Class departure lounge at Heathrow airport.

There was actually a pretty good atmosphere as all the members of the team gathered. With Joanne, Michelle and the people from Syco and Sony, seven women were travelling together with Andy. He called us his netball team. Michelle was excited because it was the first time she'd 'turned left' on a plane, and I'm still a bit apprehensive before I fly, so it's my natural instinct to try to mask the tension by joking around. As we walked down the tunnel to the plane, our footsteps spontaneously fell into sync and for some reason we all started humming Colonel Hathi's march from *The Jungle Book*! The air stewards must have wondered what on earth was coming on board!

We arrived at Narita at nine in the morning and drove into Tokyo with people from the Japanese end of Sony, who had come to greet us at the airport. The countryside very quickly disappears as you drive into the industrialized cityscape, with buildings as far as the eye can see and motorways on stilts winding their way through the urban jungle. Whizzing round the fast-moving freeways feels almost like being in a science-fiction movie. Occasionally a park appears like a verdant oasis, with boating lakes reflecting the sunshine and flowering trees laden with buds. The people from Sony were excited because the cherry blossom was due to flower any day, possibly even when we were there. There's something rather nice about top executives who work in concrete-and-glass towers talking proudly about their cherry-blossom trees. In the distance we could see the unmistakable outline of snow-capped Mount Fuji. They told us this was a very good omen.

The Ritz Carlton Hotel where we were staying is in the tallest building in Tokyo and the lift from reception shot up forty-five floors, making my ears pop. In the hotel corridors there was the usual densely carpeted luxury that made it feel much like any other posh hotel I've been in, but when I opened the door to my room, the view took my breath away. The entire far wall of the room was window, like a giant television screen, with city stretching as far as the eye could see.

It's very difficult to adjust to a different time zone, so I didn't manage to get much sleep. I was trying desperately to keep my nerves under control, but the next morning, when I was due to go to my rehearsal with the full orchestra, I was suddenly struck by a tornado of self-doubt.

I didn't know how to sing with an orchestra!

This wasn't just any orchestra, it was one of the best orchestras in the world!

It was crazy even to think of going to the rehearsal!

I couldn't understand how anyone could have thought that I could do it and it made me very angry when people tried to reassure me. Yvie tried to be strict with me, telling me that I would ruin my voice with all the crying, but even that made no difference. What did it matter if I ruined my voice? I wasn't going to go out there and sing.

It took endless patience for Andy to persuade me to go along to the concert hall. I didn't have to sing, he assured me. I didn't even have to talk to anyone. I could just sit there, or hide behind a pillar if I really wanted, just to hear how the orchestra sounded. What harm could it do? We'd come all this way. It would be a shame not even to listen.

We drove to the Metropolitan Art Space, a large concert hall where the Yomiuri Orchestra was rehearsing. Even backstage, they sounded brilliant and I couldn't resist having a wee peep inside the concert hall. There were just a few production people dotted about the stalls. The two tiers of seats above were empty. The acoustics made the sound of the orchestra full, rich and mellow. Yvie was standing just below the orchestra making notes on the score as they played and occasionally conferring with the conductor, who was dressed casually in a butter-yellow polo shirt and black trousers. He didn't look very scary at all.

Andy and I slipped surreptitiously into seats at the back of the stalls. The orchestra struck up 'Who I Was Born to Be'. As the music floated around me, all the raging tempests seemed to settle. It's such a familiar tune, it felt bizarre to hear it being played by professional violinists, cellists, percussionists, wood-wind, brass, even a harp!

'It's my song,' I whispered to Andy.

The words began to flow softly from my lips as if I had no choice but to sing it.

'Don't sing to me!' Andy hissed, exasperated. 'Get up there and do it!'

'All right then,' I told him, gathering my courage. 'I'll give it a go.'

The stage was quite high above the stalls and Andy had to hoist me up. It wasn't the most dignified way to greet the conductor, but he was a very nice man with a gentle smile. Without further ado, he tapped his baton.

As I heard the orchestra behind me playing the opening notes and I filled my lungs, it was as if I had been in pieces and was now whole again. I could do it! The relief was so exhilarating, I couldn't stop myself doing a little jig of joy during the orchestral bars building up to the final chorus. At the end of the song the orchestra applauded me, which was a fantastic feeling. We went straight into 'I Dreamed a Dream', and after that 'Wings to Fly', the song that means so much to Japanese people. It was as if I'd been singing in front of an orchestra all my life.

'I want to do it again!' I exclaimed in the people-carrier on the way back to the hotel. I was buzzing with the wonderful high of performance, but as I turned round to beam at everyone, I could see they were totally shattered by the effort of getting me there.

'You are the girl with the curl, aren't you?' said Yvie, with a smile.

Every artist pays tribute to their fans, but in my case I really wouldn't be here without them. Yes, I could hold a note. Yes, I had the nerve to risk making a fool of myself on *Britain's Got Talent*, but my story really began with the hundred million people who watched my audition on YouTube, breaking all records, and making my face so well known that the two elderly Japanese ladies who were sitting next to me and Andy in the noodle bar where we had lunch knew my name and wanted a photo.

Note to self: Udon noodles are not the best choice of food if you have false teeth and people are staring at you!

That afternoon I spent some time with a group of fans so dedicated that they had come to Tokyo to see my concert from as far away as America, Canada and Australia. When Syco got wind on the forum that this was happening, they thought how nice it would be for me to meet them, so they arranged for us to have tea together at the hotel.

What a great bunch of people! As I walked into the suite, with its panoramic view of the city, I was embraced by their warmth and good humour. They were all wearing pink badges that they had made for the occasion, printed with images of me and the Budokan and cherry blossom, and they all had red scarves, just as the fans had done when I sang in Rockefeller Plaza. Some of them had actually been there on that chilly November morning when I launched my album. In fact, two of the ladies had met for the first time in Rockefeller Plaza that day even though they live only three streets away from each other in Atlanta, Georgia. It is very heartwarming to hear that people have become friends because of me.

I said hello to each person individually and tried to

find out a little bit about their stories. Some were retired, like Linda, the lady who coordinated the trip. She didn't look nearly old enough to be retired, but she told me that being a fan of mine had made her retirement wonderful. Others had jobs from which they'd had to take time off in order to come to Tokyo. One lady said she'd had a hard time persuading her management to allow her to come, but she'd stuck up for herself.

I began to get the sense that seeing me having the courage to go for it at my audition somehow gave these women courage too. I tried to hold on to that thought so that it would make me brave when it came to the concert.

Lisa, the lady who calls herself my greatest fan, was also there. Her husband and four children were all on holiday in the Cayman Islands, but she had chosen to come to Japan instead. I was worried about what her husband would think about this, but she reassured me that he understood. Apparently he'd said, 'That girl has more moxy than anyone else, and if anyone's worth supporting, then she is.'

I'm still not sure what moxy is, but I think it's probably a good thing!

I was showered with thoughtful gifts and presented with a most beautiful bouquet of long-stemmed red roses. When a huge cake covered in strawberries and cream was wheeled in and everyone sang 'Happy Birthday', it was all I could do to stop myself crying.

There were an awful lot of candles on that cake, but my breathing exercises came in useful again, because I managed to blow them all out in one go.

'Make a wish!' they chorused, but I felt so blessed at that moment, it would have been wrong to wish for anything more.

I woke up with a start in the early hours, taking a split second to recognize my surroundings. What on earth? An enormous, king-size bed. Where on earth? Tokyo. Why on earth? It was my birthday and . . . Oh my God! I turned over and pulled the duvet over my head, trying to fool myself into going back to sleep. It didn't work.

As I lay there watching the dawn break over the city, I thought back to my last birthday, 1 April 2009. I'd woken up in the room where I had slept since I was a child, with nothing planned at all. I couldn't recall if I'd actually seen anyone that day. The only thing that had been special about it was the secret knowledge that I was going to be appearing on *Britain's Got Talent*. At that stage I'd never seen the tape of my audition. I had no idea what it would be like.

At breakfast, Andy told me that I had received a royalty cheque overnight. I didn't ask how much because money was the last thing I wanted to think about, but he said it would definitely be enough to get the white piano I'd always wanted. The next surprise was when Alex from Syco came to wish me happy birthday with a gift from Simon Cowell – a beautiful bracelet made of white gold and diamonds.

'I'm never going to take it off my wrist!' I told her.

'Ahh, isn't that lovely!' she said.

'It's not so much lovely as I don't want it to get nicked!' I told her. 'Anyone who wants this will have to chop my arm off!'

In an effort to take my mind away from the impending concert, we went out sightseeing.

The cherry-blossom season had officially started. For Japanese people, the flowering of the cherry blossom is a metaphor for the fleeting nature of life, and for one week before the petals begin to fall like drifts of delicate snow, cherry-blossom fever grips the city. People celebrate with cherry-blossom viewing parties underneath the blossom-laden boughs. On my birthday, it seemed as if the whole of Tokyo was out walking in the park. I had my picture taken a hundred times under a canopy of the palest pink blossom.

We visited another of Tokyo's famous sights, the Shibuya crossing, a six-way intersection of streets, where everyone is on the move, and the buildings glitter with constantly changing electronic images. It couldn't have been more of a contrast with the almost-sacred tranquillity of the Imperial Palace gardens, yet it felt as typically Japanese.

With my mind absorbed in the traditions of a totally different culture, the hours between breakfast and lunch flew past, but as the concert drew closer a very familiar and terrible feeling of ice-cold dread began to trickle through my veins.

The Budokan is a stadium built for martial arts during the Tokyo Olympics in 1964, and it is still used for that purpose, but it has also become a legendary venue for rock concerts. Not only the Beatles played there, but so did Bob Dylan and David Bowie. More recently, it has hosted performers as diverse as Céline Dion and Judas Priest. It is situated just on the other side of the Imperial Palace from the gardens we had visited that morning, and the car had to move slowly because of the crowds thronging the glorious cherry-blossom avenue.

We arrived in the early afternoon and I did a rehearsal with the orchestra while the vast stadium was empty. Everything was going fine until a couple of hours before I was due to perform. Just as Michelle was beginning to apply my make-up, I was suddenly overwhelmed by the enormity of what was facing me.

When you're in a dressing room backstage, you still get a sense of the arena filling up even though you can't see it. You can feel the anticipation growing. The first half of the concert included three Japanese stars of the opera and music world, singing popular arias from *Carmen*, *Aida* and *Miss Saigon*. The minutes ticked away. Michelle put my make-up on. I cried it off. Michelle put it on again. The seconds ticked away.

Finally, it was time. Andy was standing at my dressing-room door. I knew that ultimately the choice was mine. I could run away now and get the next flight home, or I could go out and show everyone what I was made of. I tried to imagine the smiling faces of all the Japanese people who had shown me so much respect and kindness; I tried to envisage my red-scarfed ladies who'd come from all corners of the globe and were waiting excitedly in the stalls. I looked at Andy who'd put in so much work to get me to the place I was now, and at Yvie who'd shown such professional dedication at a time of personal grief. They were both waiting patiently for me to be ready, perhaps wondering if I ever would be.

I took a deep breath, and nodded at Andy to take me to the stage.

Some people would think that stepping on to the stage was the easy bit, but my knees were knocking as I walked across to the mic. The lights were very bright. I couldn't see the far reaches of the stadium, but I had a sense of the thousands of faces out there looking at me. Most people would think that opening your mouth to sing to a crowd of nine thousand was the difficult bit, but as soon as I heard the music all my fears and worries ebbed away. Amazingly, there was no croakiness in my voice as I went straight into 'I Dreamed a Dream'. It sounded very powerful with the stadium full and the orchestra blasting behind me. The crowd was much bigger than any I had sung to

378

before, and the energy coming from the audience as they applauded gave my spirits a great fillip. As I started singing 'Who I Was Born to Be', I began to relax and become aware of the red scarves waving just to my left. The words of the song soared out like a rallying cry. This is what I was born to do.

I went off to get a few sips of water before returning to the stage to sing 'Amazing Grace', but I cannot tell you how that song sounded because I was trying so hard to contain all the emotion that welled up inside me. Just five days before, I had sung the same hymn without accompaniment to a small, sad congregation in a wee grey stone church on the other side of the world. I looked down into the stalls. Yvie was in her usual position just below me, her sweet face tilted heavenwards, almost as if she was trying to keep the tears in her eyes.

At the end of the hymn, nine thousand people applauded, but the two of us exchanged a poignant smile, both knowing who we were thinking about.

My final number was 'Wings to Fly'. It is a much higher, more floaty song and requires a different placement of the voice. For the first time in the evening, I squeaked the first couple of notes, but fortunately was able to correct myself. I could tell that the audience were on my side, even with that mistake, and that made me relax and enjoy the words:

Want to spread my wings and fly
Away into the sky
How I dream to be so free
No more sadness no more pain
No more anger no more hate
How I dream to have those wings and fly into the
*   sky*

The best surprise of all came after my performance when the presenter of the show was interviewing me through an interpreter. What she was saying sounded like 'Blaa blaa blaa Susan Boyle, blaa blaa blaa Susan Boyle!'

Then the orchestra unexpectedly struck up behind me. It took a moment for me to recognize the tune and to realize that the whole stadium was now singing to me.

Happy Birthday to you!
Happy Birthday to you!
Happy Birthday, dear Susan!
Happy Birthday to you!

39

Rosary

Over the last year I have been lucky enough to receive many wonderful gifts, far too many to list here. All the flowers and balloons and toys are fantastic; the albums of messages and prayers have meant a great deal to me and brought me comfort in times of stress; and I am constantly surprised and delighted by the hand-made gifts that people have put so much thought and effort into, such as the very detailed and accurate pencil drawing of me and my mother which a disabled girl had copied from the photograph she'd seen on the internet. I'd like to thank everyone who has thought about me and prayed for me for your incredible kindness and generosity.

In May 2010 I returned once again to St Bennet's, this time to receive a very special presentation. In the beautiful little oratory, His Eminence asked a lovely lady called Maria Dorrian to explain the extraordinary story of how a set of rosary beads had been created specially for me.

Maria works in Scotland for St Padre Pio's Friary, which is in San Giovanni Rotondo, Puglia, in Italy. She is a fan of mine and one day last year she was involved in a thread on one of my fan sites where my faith was being discussed. Maria continued the conversation with a volunteer from the Marian Information Center in Las Vegas, who expressed interest in bringing the relics of Padre Pio to Las Vegas. From that introduction, Maria accompanied the relics to many churches there and met the Bishop of Las Vegas and members of the congregation.

As the link in this spiritual journey that people from different sides of the world were experiencing was Susan Boyle (although I knew nothing about it at the time), the idea of the rosary was conceived. The Marian group in Las Vegas asked their members each to supply one bead from their own rosary, with other beads coming from Maria herself and from her close friends in Scotland, Holland, California and Connecticut.

Maria then contacted Cardinal O'Brien to ask him if he would give a bead from his rosary too. He gave one from the rosary on which he'd prayed at the Vatican while awaiting his audience with Pope Benedict XVI.

A lady called Collette from Nevada took all the beads and created an exquisite rosary, which includes a silver locket containing a piece of cloth that covered the wounds of Padre Pio's stigmata. The crucifix is from the shrine of Medjugorje in Bosnia-Herzegovina. The rosary was blessed at the tomb of St Padre Pio.

Maria invited the Cardinal to present me with the rosary and, accompanying it, a leather-bound book with a handwritten message from each donor, promising to pray for me in my singing vocation. I was overcome with emotion to hold in my hands the product of so many prayers from people around the world. Using my unique and precious new rosary, we recited the five decades and sang hymns to Our Lady. At the Cardinal's request, I sang 'Ave Maria', pouring all my gratitude and humility into the prayer.

Afterwards there was a lovely tea laid out for us. As we relaxed and chatted, Friar GianMaria, who had travelled from Padre Pio's shrine in southern Italy, said that God uses certain humble people, often from insignificant little towns, to make a spiritual impact on the world and that I was one of those people who leads people to God and Our Lady.

'I haven't done anything!' I protested.

I'm just an ordinary person, but I have always believed that I am on a path that God has created for me, so if this path is one that brings people together, then I am very glad and grateful to Him.

40

Moving On

As I come to the end of my memoir, I am sitting in the living room of Yule Terrace where I have always lived, trying to pluck up the courage to make another journey, to my own new house. It is in Blackburn, where I feel at home, but I'll have more space for a piano, and it's somewhere I'll feel safer. I was a wee bit spooked when a lad broke into my house earlier this year, and my family and friends keep telling me that I'm too vulnerable in Yule Terrace.

There are so many memories all around me here, especially of my beloved mother. I often find myself wondering what she would have made of it all. I know she would have been so proud of me recording an album and singing with an orchestra in Japan, but she would have been equally delighted by the generosity and support I've been shown closer to home. In June, in the nearby village of Polbeth, I was invited to the Gala Day to crown the wee Gala Day Queen. Gala Days are joyous occasions for the local community, and it meant a lot to me to be asked to play a part. It was a beautiful sunny day as well, and I felt as if I spent the whole time smiling. I know that would have made my mother very happy.

Somebody told me recently that I had come seventh in a poll of the most influential people in the world. I suspect the result was swung by some of my more ardent fans voting fast and often, but how daft can you get? As I sit here in my living room, I can almost see my mother's face lighting up at that news and hear her peals of laughter.

But I have learned that you can't hold on to memories for ever because that is like holding on to the person and preventing them from enjoying the life that God has prepared for them.

> *And so here am I*
> *Open arms and ready to stand*
> *I've got the world in my hands*
> *And it feels like my turn to fly.*
>
> *And though I may not*
> *Know the answers*
> *I can finally say I'm free*
> *And if the questions*
> *Lead me here, then*
> *I am who I was born to be.*

There are still many questions I constantly ask

myself. Am I doing things right? Am I becoming a better person?

In a way, this first year has been my growing up. I was innocent at the start, and I was unprotected. I probably received more attention than any other unelected person for many years. I accept that it goes with the job, but at times it was an almost unbearable pressure.

Now I have people around me that I trust and am willing to be guided by. My confidence is growing and with it, I hope, my professionalism. I like to think I have become more of a lady.

I still have my moments of doubt. Doesn't everybody? That's only human. I know there's still a long way to go in my evolving journey.

I want to continue to grow as an entertainer myself and become better at it, but I am also starting to look at different avenues to explore, like seeing if there are ways I can give other struggling artists the chance to achieve their dreams.

Some of the most satisfying moments this year have been when I have been asked to sing to help other people, such as recording the single in aid of the rescue effort in Haiti, and performing 'Wild Horses' for Sport Relief. I hope I will be able to do more charity work, giving financially and benefiting those who have a disability.

If there is one thing I would most like to think I have achieved this past year, it is to have made life a little easier for people with a disability. In my dictionary there's no such word as 'disability'. Those first three letters imply that you're limited, that a fence has been built around you – not by you, but by what people think of you. If you take those first three letters off, then you've got 'ability', and the gate is open.

You should always focus on what you can do, not on what you can't do – and remember, there's no rush. People want things straight away these days and there's a lot of pressure to get on, but some people need a bit more time to fulfil their potential.

If my story means anything, it is that people are very often too quick to judge a person by the way they look or by their quirks of behaviour. I may not have quite the same sense of humour as other people, but at least I do have a sense of humour, and I've needed it! As a society, we seem to have very tight restrictions on what is considered 'normal'. I am happy to admit that I have had some difficulties, but I also have many blessings: the gift of a voice that makes people happy; the certainty of my faith in an uncertain world.

I hope that my story demonstrates that you shouldn't just look at the label, you should always look at the whole person, emotionally, physically, mentally and spiritually.

One of the things that is most different about my life now is that I never know what is going to happen next. If my life was a wee bit monochrome before, now it is a rainbow of colour and contrast. I've learned to embrace and relish that uncertainty instead of fearing it. In the past few weeks, I have been offered a guest role as dinner lady in the hit American television series *Glee*; I have also received an invitation to sing for the Pope when he visits Scotland in September. The first would be great fun, the second would be a privilege and an honour so profound I could never even have dreamed of wishing for it.

As my friend Frank Quinn has said on many occasions, 'You are writing your story, Susan. It's about achievement and belief in yourself.'

I have no idea what the next chapter is going to be, but I do know that I'm looking forward to whatever the future holds.

A Reflection

God of New Beginnings
I come before You with an open heart and
*   outstretched arms*
Seeking guidance as I reach beyond myself
To find your love in everyone I meet and everyone I
*   sing for.*
I ask that my arms might embrace your Spirit
And that my eyes continue to see You in others
As I celebrate your love.
I ask for the strength and patience to be a person of
*   peace and an instrument*
For justice and respect for all people, especially
*   people with a disability.*
I wish to keep my life simple and always keep in
*   mind the simplicity of your message: Your love*
*   for all of us.*
Through your divine strength I open in a new way,
Committing myself to always try and walk your
*   path and share in your work.*
I thank You for the gift of people, the talents of all
*   people and my own gift of music and song.*
It is through respecting each other that we
*   experience oneness with You.*
Keep me close and never let me stray from You.
Let me always be a person of hope and certain of
*   your powerful and gentle presence.*

Amen

Acknowledgements

I would like to express my gratitude to everyone who has been involved in my story, especially to each and every one of my family, my friends and my fantastic fans.

I am especially grateful to my sisters Mary and Bridie, and my nieces Kirsty, Joanne and Pamela for sharing their memories for this book. Kirsty and Joanne have been a great support throughout the year, and I want to thank them very much for that.

I would like to thank Lorraine Campbell and Fred O'Neil for contributing to the book. I am also grateful to Charles Earley for supplying details about the West Lothian Voluntary Arts Council.

I am grateful to Mark Lucas and the team at LAW, and to Doug Young and everyone at Transworld who has been involved in the publication of my book.

Thank you Ossie for organizing everything so well.

Thank you Yvie and Steve for your professional expertise and friendship.

I am indebted to my friend and teacher Frank Quinn who has cheered and inspired me and to His Eminence Cardinal Keith Patrick O'Brien for his support and hospitality.

I am very fortunate indeed to have Andy Stephens as my manager and I am constantly grateful for his good sense, good humour and great company. Thanks, Andy!

Finally, my heartfelt thanks go to Imogen Parker, whose patience, sensitivity and sense of humour made the daunting task of telling my story a very enjoyable experience.

Index

Aidan 223, 284, 315
Alex 347, 376
'Amazing Grace' 326–7, 367, 379
America's Got Talent 333, 335–8
Ant and Dec 16–17, 215, 297
'Ave Maria' 173, 312, 383

'Babes in the Wood' 38–9
Bakie, Miss 122–3
Bangour Hospital 23, 122–3
Banjo, Ashley 275
Barnum 159
Barrymore, Michael 160–2, 238
Bathgate Menzies Choir 188
Bay City Rollers 110
Beatles 9, 334
Bernadette, Saint 72–4, 129
Bill and Ben the Flower Pot Men 50
Black, Cilla 37
Blackburn 26–7
Blackburn Community Centre 132
Blackburn, Tony 98–9
Bowling Club (Blackburn) 148, 170–1
Box Office, The 189
Boyle, Bridget (Bridie) (mother) 27, 28–9, 34, 35, 128, 176–7, 235, 329, 356
background 49, 92
birth of Susan 23–5
and cats 177–8
death 201–2
death of brother 195
death of daughter (Kathleen) 195
death of husband 181–2
decline in health 195–6, 200
during war 49
fount of knowledge 89–90, 176
love of reading 48
marriage 49
and painting 176–7
piano playing 35
relationship with Susan 29, 45–6, 128, 145–6, 234–5, 328–9
religious beliefs 43–6, 72, 79, 81
sense of humour 50
and singing 36
Boyle, Bridie (sister) 26–7, 30–1, 37, 61, 109–10, 195–6, 202, 219–20, 228
Boyle, Gerard (brother) 27, 36, 71, 88, 101, 102–3, 116–17, 228, 258
Boyle, James (brother) 27, 88

Boyle, Joe (brother) 27, 32, 37, 88

Boyle, John (brother) 27, 36, 88, 101, 202, 258,

Boyle, Kathleen (sister) 27, 61, 64, 87–8, 101, 183–5, 195

Boyle, Mary (sister) 26–7, 28, 32, 36, 103, 108

Boyle, Patricia (sister) 25

Boyle, Patrick (father) 26–7, 68, 141, 175–6
  Celtic FC supporter 62–3, 362
  death 180–1
  during war 35–6, 49
  ill-health 179–80
  marriage 49
  relationship with Susan 146–8, 328–9
  religious beliefs 43–5, 181
  and singing 35–6, 47, 70, 175
  upbringing of children 32

Boyle, Susan
  Early Years and Life Before ***Britain's Got Talent***
    baptism and confirmation 28, 87
    birth and slight brain damage suffered 23–5, 42, 59
    bullying at school 57–8, 110, 111–14, 115
    childhood and house brought up in Blackburn 26, 28, 39–40, 41–2, 43–4, 67
    Christmases 100–2
    church attendance 43–6
    course in caring 195, 197–200
    crush on Donny Osmond 97–9
    depression suffered and referral to psychologist 118, 119, 121–2
    at Edinburgh Acting School 157–8, 159
    fainting fits 116

    First Communion 74–7
    first visit to Lourdes and impact of trip 128–31
    health problems and hospital visits 32–4, 51, 57
    holidays in Ireland 65–70, 79–81, 119–20, 166–7
    hyperactivity 34, 57, 118
    learning difficulties 34, 55–6
    musical background 35–40
    musical tastes 103
    Open University social work course 143–4
    at primary school 52–8, 71–2, 78
    and reading 48, 55, 95, 115
    at St Kentigern's Academy 105–9, 110–11
    school report card and O-grade results 78, 115
    singing at school concerts and competitions 82–6
    storywriting 95–6
    television programmes watched 50, 88–9
    trips to the seaside 46–7
    voluntary work 131–3, 143
    and Youth Opportunities Scheme 120
  Personal Life
    birthday 375
    boyfriend 146–8
    Celtic FC supporter 62–4, 362
    charity work 386
    crowns Gala Day Queen at Polbeth 384
    death of father 180–1
    death of mother and coping on own 18, 200–5
    death of sister (Kathleen) 183–5
    drawbacks on being a celebrity 318, 351–2, 357–8
    fear of flying 220–1, 332–3

given quilt by American fans
345–6
joins Legion of Mary 204
loneliness brought about by
fame 239, 265
love of theatre and musicals
157, 159–60
lunch with Cardinal O'Brien
and singing of 'Ave
Maria' 307–12
meeting of Donny Osmond
340–1
and mimicry 9, 50, 94, 158
and mother's decline in
health 196, 200
musical tastes 159–60
'never been kissed' comment
16, 281
opportunities given due to
celebrity 358–63
parental background 26–7,
49, 91
and Pebbles (cat) 182, 203,
233–4, 261, 357
presented with
specially–made rosary
381–3
Priory stay 301–3, 317
relationship with father 146,
147–8, 328–9
relationship with mother 29,
45–6, 128, 145, 235,
328–9
relationship with siblings
41–3, 178
relationship with sister
(Kathleen) 61, 87–8
religious faith 46, 72–4,
80–1, 204–5, 236–8,
257, 289, 296, 326, 383
return visit to St Kentigern
105–6, 114–15
sings at Yvie's mother's
funeral 366–8
visit to Universal Studios
339
visits convent of Daughters

of Charity of St Vincent
de Paul in Paris 352–3
Singing Career
American trips 333–9,
343–6
annual talent showcases
189–90, 205–6
and *Britain's Got Talent* see
Britain's Got Talent
(2009)
and *Britain's Got Talent*
tour 314–16
Christmas television special
354–6
contribution to Whitburn's
Millennium CD 186–8
Dancing with the Stars
performance 339–40
debut on *America's Got
Talent* 330, 333, 335–8
developing of repertoire
168, 170
and fans 60, 372–5, 381
feelings when singing 140,
257, 324, 325
guest role in *Glee* 388
invitation to sing for the
Pope during Scottish
visit 388
Japanese trip to sing with
orchestra at Budokan
364–5, 368–80
joins Toccata Ladies Choir
190
karaoke nights 170
launching of debut album
live on *Today Show*
342–5
makeup and costumes for
performances 335–7,
348–9
managed by Andy Stephens
317–18, 336
My Kind of People audition
160–2
Opportunity Knocks
audition 153–5

Boyle, Susan (*cont.*)
  photographic shoot for
    Harper's Bazaar 77
  presented with triple
    platinum album 356
  recording of first album and
    promotion of in Europe
    319–30, 331, 347–52
  recording of first tracks
    171–2
  singing competitions 150–1,
    160, 172–3
  singing with Elaine Paige
    highlight 355
  singing lessons with O'Neil
    163–9
  sings 'Ave Maria' in church
    173–4
  sings in Paris 342
  sings socially in clubs
    138–41, 148–51, 170
  stagefright and nerves 86,
    273–4, 293–4, 333,
    343–5, 370, 377–8
  takes part in Millennium
    Celebration Concert
    (2000) 187–9
  team behind 317–18, 347–9
  warm-up singing exercises
    337, 350
  wiggle on stage 18, 214,
    223, 227, 263, 276
Britain's Got Talent (2007) 206
Britain's Got Talent (2009)
  American television
    appearances 239–40
  audition 10–19, 211–16
  backlash against and criticism
    of 277, 297
  fame and celebrity status 227,
    228–33, 255–6
  family reactions 258
  feelings on losing final
    298–300
  final 293–8
  inner turmoil and struggle
    under pressure 257, 259,
    271, 281–3, 294–5
  interviews 221, 232–5
  lack of sleep and exhaustion
    255, 271, 272, 284, 287,
    293–4, 298, 301
  makeover debate 235–6
  media frenzy and press
    harassment 229–33, 237,
    241–7, 264–5, 266,
    279–82, 291–2
  outbursts 282, 295
  picked for semi-finals 221–4
  seeks sanctuary from press in
    church 287–90
  semi-final 261–76
  support and fan adulation
    236, 293
  tabloid stories 234–6, 238,
    281–4
  view of Diversity and other
    performers 275–6, 284,
    298
  voice coaching 249–52, 271–2
  and YouTube 231, 235, 238,
    372
Britain's Got Talent Tour
    314–16
Brookstein, Steve 191
Budokan (Tokyo) 365, 377
Buncrana (Ireland) 119
Burnett, Yvie 248–54, 268, 271,
    295–6, 319–20, 337,
    349–50, 366–8, 370–1, 372,
    379
Byrne, Mrs 78

Caine, Marti 153
Campbell, Lorraine 83, 85, 229,
    232, 266–70, 277–80,
    285–8, 291–2, 295
Campbell, Stephen 105–6
Celtic Football Club 62–3, 362
Clarkson, Kelly 327
Cowell, Simon 17–19, 190–1,
    214–15, 223–4, 271, 275,
    291, 294, 298, 329, 376
Crackerjack 88–9

Crawford, Michael 159–60
Crowther, Leslie 88–9
'Cry Me a River' 168, 187, 189, 238, 324
Curran, John 189

Dancing with the Stars 339–40
Danesh, Darius 191
Daughters of Charity of St Vincent de Paul (Paris) 352–3
'Daydream Believer' 327
Dermot, Father 288–90
Disneyland 335
Diversity 262, 275, 284, 298, 315
Dixon, Barbara 355
Donegal (Ireland) 79
Dorrian, Maria 381–3
Dupe 288–90

Earley, Charles 187, 189, 205
Edinburgh 133–4, 155
Edinburgh Acting School 157–9, 274
Edinburgh Playhouse 159–60
Edmonds, Noel 153
Escala 275

Faces of Disco 262, 276
Fallon, Sister Patricia 361
Fanshawe, Simon 156
Flawless 284, 315, 316
Frankie (runner) 232, 252, 266

Gala Days 149–50
Gascoigne, Bamber 89
Gates, Gareth 191
Gemmell, Tommy 362
Gerry and the Pacemakers 38
GianMaria, Friar 383
Glaze, Peter 89
Glee 388
Good Morning America 235
Goodman, Len 339–40
Grease 118
Green, Mr 78, 82–5

Grey, Cardinal Joseph 87

Hadley, Tony 359
Haiti rescue effort 386
Happy Valley, The (Blackburn) 137, 148, 170
Harper's Bazaar 77
Hatch, Tony 153
Heartbeat Studio 171, 324
Hell, Nick 262, 276
Holden, Amanda 17, 213–14, 215, 275
Hopkin, Mary 152
Hotel Bel-Air 334
'How Great Thou Art' 326

'I Don't Know How to Love Him' 109, 139, 154–5, 162, 172, 238
'I Dreamed A Dream' 18, 19, 206, 211–12, 294, 325, 340, 378
'I Know Him So Well' 170, 355

Jackson, Darth 262, 276, 315, 316
Jackson, La Toya 351
Jackson, Leon 193
Jackson, Michael death of 315
Japan Susan's trip to 368–80
Joanne (niece) 202, 241–6, 271, 338–9
John Paul II, Pope 127, 134–5, 309, 352
Julian (saxophonist) 298

Kavanagh, Mr 133
Kelly, Charles 85
Kemp brothers 359
Kilkenny, Ossie 317
Kirsty (niece) 88, 260, 271, 317
Knock (Ireland) 79–81, 129

Laine, Frankie 36
Larry King Live 239–40

Locke, Josef 36
Loreto, Sister 352–3
Lourdes 72–4, 129–31

Mac, Steve 322, 323, 325–6,
    328, 331
McAleese, President Mary 310
McCartney, Paul 37
McGregor, Kerry 191
McLaughlin, Granny 91–2
McLaughlin, John 91
McLaughlin, Michael 34, 46,
    90–4, 119, 176, 184, 195,
    301–2
McManus, Michelle 191
McNulty, Father Michael 28, 72,
    74
Madonna 114, 327
Marian Information Center (Las
    Vegas) 382
Marzella, Marco 188
Marzella, Michael 188
'Memory' 261
Michelle (make–up lady) 348–9,
    368, 377
Millennium 186
Millennium CD 186–7, 238
Millennium Celebration Concert
    (2000) 187–9
Misérables, Les 160, 206
Molly (Yvie's mother) 254, 320,
    366–7
Monaghan, Mrs 53–4
Monkees 327
Morgan, Piers 17, 18, 213, 214,
    233, 239–40, 272, 274–5,
    283–4, 297, 337
Murphy, James 137
Murphy, Jim 361
'My Heart Must Go On' 170
My Kind of People 160–2

Naidenko, Julia 262
Neville, Suzanne 335, 349
New Faces 153

Obama, President 256

O'Brien, Cardinal Keith Patrick
    237, 307–12, 361–2, 381–3
O'Doherty, Mrs 67, 70
Okri, Natalie 223, 224, 262,
    275
O'Neil, Fred 162, 163–9, 250
Opportunity Knocks 152–3
Osborne, Sharon 337
Osmond, Donny 97–99, 100,
    102, 340–1
Osmonds 98–99, 102
Our Lady of Lourdes church
    (Blackburn) 43, 44–5, 80
Our Lady of Lourdes Primary
    School 52, 71–2, 82
Our Lady, Queen of Ireland
    church (Knock) 80

Paige, Elaine 159, 261, 355–6
Pamela (niece) 88, 183–4, 204,
    241–7, 302–3
Polbeth Gala Day 384
Pop Idol 191
Portrush (Ireland) 66–9, 166
Potts, Paul 206
Priory, The 301–3, 317
'Proud' 328–9

Quinn, Frank 135, 194–5,
    196–9, 232, 257, 259,
    294–5, 326, 388

Raymonde, Nick 322
Reid, Trina 162
Ritz Carlton hotel (Tokyo)
    369–70
Robinson, Anne 350
Rogers, Carl
    On Becoming a Person 142
Royal Hospital for Sick Children
    33, 51

St Bennet's 307–12, 381
St Joseph's (Rosewell) 135
St Kentigern's Academy 105–8,
    111, 114–15, 117
Sawyer, Diane 235–6

'Scarlet Ribbons' 47
Second World War 49
Shadows 36
Shaheen 281, 315
Simpsons, The 249
Son, Sue 262, 275
Sonny and Cher 37
Sony 348, 364, 368–9
Sound of Music, The 36, 86
Sounds of West Lothian (CD)
    186–7, 188, 238
Spandau Ballet 359
Sport Relief 386
Springfield, Dusty 37
Stavros Flatley 284, 316, 351
Steel, Hollie 315
Stein, Jock 62
Stein, Mrs 58
Stephens, Andy 258, 317–18,
    336, 344, 370–1, 378
Stewart, Allan 359–60
Stewart, Ed 153
Strictly Come Dancing 339
'Summer Nights' 118
Syco 319, 322, 368

Talkback Thames 232
Tam O'Shanter Club (Coventry)
    148
'That Lucky Old Sun' 36
That's Life 156
Toccata Ladies Choir 190
Today Show 342–5
Top of the Pops 37, 43, 99

Turf, The (Blackburn) 170

Universal Studios 339
University Challenge 89
'Up to the Mountain' 327

Webber, Andrew Lloyd 159, 261
Wembley Arena 314
West Lothian Voluntary Arts
    Council 189, 205, 206
Whelan, Francis 173
Whitburn Community Council
    186
Whitburn Miners' Welfare Club
    150, 172
'Who I Was Born to Be' 327,
    371, 379
'Wild Horses' 252, 329–30, 338,
    342, 386
Winfrey, Oprah 249
'Wings to Fly' 364, 372, 379–80
Winter of Discontent 121
Wogan, Terry 94–5
Woodentops, The 50

X Factor, The 191–2, 249, 342

Yomiuri Orchestra 371–2
'You'll Never Walk Alone' 38
'You'll See' 114, 327
Young, Will 191
YouTube 231, 235, 238, 372

Zavaroni, Lena 152